THE CHALLENGE OF RELIGIOUS STUDIES

Kenneth G. Howkins
foreword by John W. Alexander

InterVarsity Press
Downers Grove, Illinois 60515

Second printing,
January 1975
© 1972 by
Tyndale Press, London.
First American printing,
June 1973, by
InterVarsity Press with
permission from
Inter-Varsity Fellowship,
England.

InterVarsity Press is
the book publishing
division of Inter-Varsity
Christian Fellowship.

ISBN 0-87784-714-2
Library of Congress Catalog
Card Number: 73-75896

Printed in the United
States of America

Contents

Should we demythologize?
Being up to date
Miracles, science and history

Foreword
to the
American Edition

Today more than ever before, courses in religion are being offered in all kinds of universities, public as well as private, nonsectarian as well as Protestant and Catholic. Those who register have a variety of religious beliefs. Some are totally committed to biblical Christianity. Some are skeptics looking for more reasons not to believe. Some are confused but searching and longing for something to give meaning to their shattered lives.

Put students of various backgrounds and goals together with a teacher whose background and goals are different yet and you have a charged atmosphere. More heat than light may result.

Professor Kenneth G. Howkins recognizes this situation and has written *The Challenge of Religious Studies* to help students caught in this particular impasse. He takes up the question of how a person of one persuasion can learn and profit from a course of instruction which is often at odds with his own faith. And he helps students understand how every man's "knowledge" of religious truth relies on presuppositions. It isn't the Christian alone who makes assumptions or relies on "faith." For the student under pressure from an unsympathetic teacher, chapter three, "Modern Approaches," can be a liberating experience.

But the book is also valuable for students whose religious commitment is less traditional. It can help any reader to recognize what presuppositions are and to examine his own presuppositions as well as those of his teachers.

Prof. Howkins has written this book primarily to students in British secondary schools and universities. Thus some of the terminology relating to the British educational system may seem foreign to American readers. But the points which the author makes are as valid for Americans as for Britishers. Perhaps, therefore, it would be helpful to review some of the peculiarities of the British system and to suggest how the principles Prof. Howkins elucidates are appropriate to the American scene.

First, although any parent can choose not to have his child participate, Religious Studies are compulsory in all state secondary schools from the first form (age 12) to the fourth form (age 16) and optional through the sixth form (age 18). The close connection between church and state is the historical background for that situation. Of course, in the United States the opposite situation prevails. Until recently religion has scarcely been taught in state schools in the United States, the separation of church and state being written into the constitution.

Second, it will help to know that secondary education in Britain includes roughly the first two years of college work by American standards. When a student graduates from secondary school in Britain, he has, so to speak, a junior college education. At this point he may take exams which qualify him for entrance to the universities. One of the subjects he may choose to be examined in is Religious Studies.

Third, it has only been in the last hundred years that university education has developed much beyond the two universities of Oxford and Cambridge. But in the last few decades, not only has British education expanded in general, but Departments of Religious Studies have been multiplying and growing. Prof. Howkins takes up this subject in chapter two.

The background of religious education in American universities is equally of interest to readers of this book. We are fortunate to have Claude Welch's *Graduate Education in Religion: A Critical Appraisal* (Missoula: University of Montana Press, 1971) to rely on here. Chapter nine, "Undergraduate Studies: Growth and Redirection, 1950-1970," is filled with information on the U.S. scene comparable to that presented by Prof. Howkins in chapter two.

Perhaps the most important factor to note is that, as in Britain so in the United States, programs in religion have developed most dramatically since 1950. "By 1969-1970, nearly all the accredited four-year institutions of higher learning in the United States and Canada were offering courses in religion. . . . Approximately two-thirds of those schools had established a special program of Religious Studies" (p. 167). As Welch says, it is not surprising that the vast majority of both Protestant and Roman Catholic institutions have programs in Religious Studies, but "what is striking is that by the end of the 1960's almost half of the private nonsectarian schools and thirty percent of the public institutions had some formal program for the study of religion" (p. 167).

Welch's analysis of what is being taught in Religious Studies reads like an American rewrite of Howkins' chapter two: "A new conception of the purpose of the study of religion is evident in the rapid growth of programs in the independent and public colleges and universities. These are pluralistic in faculty, they have no intent to prepare students for clerical careers, and they eschew both evangelistic and pastoral goals" (p. 192). Furthermore, Welch notes a swing toward Eastern religions, especially courses in comparative religion which are more broadly based than the traditional courses in Judaism and Christianity. Interdepartmental studies, such as those mentioned by Howkins, are also gaining in popularity. Then too there is an enlargement of the concept of religion: Camus, D. H. Lawrence, Nietzsche, Marx and Freud are "almost as likely to appear on reading lists as Augustine and Barth" (p. 196). All in all, the differences between religious education in Britain and in the United States are becoming fewer and fewer.

From the above it might appear that the present volume is a book on education as such. This is not so. The real subject is not how Christians should react to Religious Studies but how they should study religion itself. Even if there were no connection between the way in which Americans and Britishers conduct their Religious Studies programs, readers would find real value in Prof. Howkins' treatment of miracles and the supernatural, the resurrection of Christ, biblical criticism and Christology. The important matter is not how we conduct our educational system but how we can best learn what God has for us in his Word.

Prof. Howkins reminds us of this when he writes that the purpose of biblical theology is to "find out what the Bible really says." He notes that even here it is "possible to read books about biblical theology without reading the Bible itself. The study then becomes not what the Bible says, but what various scholars say the Bible says. This is a trap as much for the lecturer as for the student." And that reminds us that our real job as Christians is to go to the source and learn from it. The present book can help us be a little more sophisticated about how we read the Bible. But if our reading of this book or any other book about the Bible takes the place of Bible study, it can only be a detriment.

It is in the spirit of honest and open inquiry that I am pleased to recommend this volume.

John W. Alexander
President
Inter-Varsity Christian Fellowship

Introduction

1

There is a natural enthusiasm and excitement in beginning a new study. There are new areas to be explored, new discoveries to be made, and new problems to be grappled with. For the committed Christian, beginning Religious Studies is an enterprise filled with hope, as the subject is so close to his heart and is a part of his life. There are, of course, those who enter the study without any personal faith, or with a confused mind, not knowing what to believe. Theirs may be a quest for faith, a desire to learn more in order to be able to make an informed choice in accepting or rejecting Christianity (or some other form of religion); or it may be simply an objective interest, a thirst for knowledge, a curiosity to find out what religion really is. It is not primarily for such that these words are written (though they may find them of interest), but for the committed Christian.

Every occupation has its hazards, and the study of Divinity, Theology, Biblical or Religious Studies, or Religious Education is no exception. Many a student has begun a course with the fond hope that it would be an extension of his own devotions, a deepening of his spiritual experience, and a heart-warming time of divine blessing. Many a student has ended a course not knowing what to believe, if anything, and finding that the joy and assurance of his Christian life have disappeared, that the Bible, once his guide and inspiration, is dead, and that prayer has no further meaning. Theology can have this effect. As T. F. Torrance said, 'Detached from the empirical reality of the living and acting God, theology tended to become abstract and rationalistic and got stuck in arid ideas and inflexible frames of thought, losing its relevance for the life of faith.'[1]

But not all students have such a naive beginning or such a disastrous ending, and this is certainly not inevitable. Nevertheless many do find that the study is a time of mental and spiritual conflict, ending, if not in disaster, at least in impoverishment.

It is for this reason that some students refuse to take up such a study, and prefer to play safe by studying another subject. Indeed there are some sincere Christians who would never intentionally read any religious book written from a point of view different from their own, either because they feel that it would be harmful to their faith, or because they think that it would have no value. Thus Hywel Jones, writing as an evangelical, laments the 'openness' of those evangelicals who find value in 'non-evangelical books'; he severely censures the attitude of 'an open mind to God's truth wherever it is found', as he considers that 'this amounts to having a closed mind to the finality, sufficiency, infallibility and authority of the Scriptures on all that they say—and they speak of everything—and an open mind to what men of secular scholarship have to say'. His view is that Scripture 'contains what God wishes us to know and believe about all that is written within its pages, such as creation and the history of mankind', and so for him an open mind should mean only 'a fearless willingness to draw *all* the conclusions of the doctrinal statements we make'. Any rethinking of traditional views he condemns as making 'concessions', and he finds 'the new evangelicals' particularly guilty in this.[2]

But the student, whose mind is being trained to think, cannot keep his religious beliefs in a sealed compartment, whatever the subject of his formal studies may be. To attempt to do so is to commit intellectual suicide, and in fact is a denial of his faith. He needs to think about his own beliefs and those of others, and thus to enlarge his understanding.

USING THE MIND

A Christian's mind belongs to God as much as any other part of his being, and it needs to be devoted to God. 'Anyone who chooses Jesus Christ as his total, undivided Lord', comments Helmut Thielicke,[3] 'should not then divide himself into a trusting heart placed at his Lord's disposal, and a critical head which he keeps for himself or—what is even worse—simply puts on ice.' Indeed, the Bible encourages the use of the mind in the practice of religion. We are commanded to love God with all our mind and understanding.[4] Again, we are urged to gird up our minds, and to be prepared to give a defence of the reason for our hope.[5]

This needs to be stressed today, as there is a certain mood of irrationalism prevailing 'which could do great damage to our spiritual integrity and our intellectual honesty'.[6] Thus Zahrnt scorns rational proofs and evidence, and tells us that 'faith carries within itself its own certainty'.[7] But this seems more like credulity than faith. It has been pointed out that because of this non-rational trend 'the depreciation of C. S. Lewis is now fashionable in certain circles'.[8]

The Christian will need to think in a Christian way about everything, and this is a long and rigorous discipline. It is particularly difficult as such a great proportion of the information and opinions he receives is from a non-Christian standpoint. He will need to think carefully whether the view of history, or politics, or society which he is accepting is really in full accord with his Christian beliefs.[9]

It is so easy to be a Christian in certain parts of one's life only. To be a Christian in a non-Christian world, or, as some would say, in a post-Christian society, inevitably means a conflict of ideas, values, motives and beliefs. The easy way out is to have a double mind, one part of which engages in private devotions, public worship and Christian fellowship, and the other part in the pursuits, the learning and the

pleasures of this world. But this is most unsatisfactory, a.
is a failure to face up to reality, and can lead to unbearable
tension. If the Christian believes that honesty is a virtue of
supreme importance, he will endeavour to apply it to himself before God, to his relationships with all other people,
to all his studies and to all his life. This is not easy, and
there is no neat and clear-cut set of answers to all the issues
that arise. But basically the Christian believes in one
supreme living God, the Creator of all, including man and
the world. There must therefore be a link in the Christian's
beliefs about God, man and the world. Christianity should
affect *all* of a Christian's thinking.

This applies also to the Christian's religious beliefs themselves, as these may well be accepted without adequate
thought. It is necessary to work out the implications in
detail of one's basic beliefs, to ensure that the whole of one's
religious beliefs accord with their basis. It is easy to slip
into a non-Christian way of thinking, even in Christian
matters. We may, for example, ask ourselves whether our
view of prayer is fully Christian, in the first place as
regards our *beliefs* about prayer, and then as regards our
practice. For it may be somewhat selfish, and perhaps almost
like a form of magic. It is because of this that the author of
Honest to God can speak of a 'daddy in the sky'. That, of
course, is a parody; but we need to beware that our prayers
are not a parody of true prayer.

Again, we may have found in the past that experience
has confirmed the claim of the Bible to be the Word of God,
and we may have benefited very greatly from reading it
regularly. We need to consider whether we are in fact thinking about the Bible in a truly Christian way, and to find the
basis for our thinking. Every Christian student embarking
on a new course of study would do well to face this issue,
before finding it thrust upon him in an overpowering manner.

USING THE BIBLE

Before He finished His earthly ministry (according to the
Fourth Gospel), Jesus instructed His disciples and warned

them to be prepared to encounter trouble : He said, 'I have told you all this to guard you against the breakdown of your faith.'[10] So the Christian needs to know both what he believes and why he believes it. The claim made constantly throughout the Bible is that the living God has revealed Himself, and that the Bible is the inspired record of that revelation. 'When in former times God spoke to our fore-fathers, he spoke in fragmentary and varied fashion through the prophets. But in this the final age he has spoken to us in the Son.'[11] This claim that an authoritative revelation has been given and recorded is seen throughout the Old Testament, and in the words attributed to Christ and His apostles. Moreover the claim is a basic part of the Christian message. The Christian student should therefore find out in detail just what this claim is, and decide whether he is prepared to submit to this authority. Such submission is not an end to thinking; rather it is a basis for thinking, and an intelligent obedience with mind and heart to the living God who has revealed Himself. More will be said of this later.

AN OPEN MIND

One piece of advice frequently given is to have an open mind. This sounds extremely plausible, but in practice it can be a very subtle form of brain-washing and indoctrina-tion. The mind needs to be open at the top, to let new ideas drop in, and not at the bottom, to let all former ideas drop out. It is as well to remember, as it has been said, that if the mind is open wide enough a great deal of rubbish will be tipped into it! The New Testament warns us of the danger of having a childish mind 'tossed to and fro and carried about with every wind of doctrine, by the cunning of men'.[12] The student needs an open mind towards those things which he does not know, and a readiness to grapple with problems. But he does not need to empty his mind of those matters about which he has a sure knowledge. He should not jettison previous knowledge but, with intellectual humility, be willing to consider other views. To have an ever-open mind in everything is simply a serious neurosis. We need to make decisions, and we need the courage to stand by our decisions. It is not a sign of maturity to be carried away by 'every eddy in the stream of thought'. The demand for an open mind is so often in practice a demand for an empty mind. Sometimes this is overtly so. There are those who ask their students to remove all preconceived ideas from their minds, and to start thinking again. This is morally very questionable. It tends to be saying in effect in an authoritarian manner, 'Abandon your beliefs and accept mine.'

A completely closed mind on any matter is not being advocated. Indeed a modification of ideas may be demanded. But it is not desirable to consider that every question is completely open. If the Christian student has known in experience that the Bible is the Word of God, and if God has spoken to him through it—if, in other words, he has found that the Bible's claims for itself make sense and authenticate themselves—then, if this is called into question, such experience will be a strong factor in weighing up the evidence. There will, of course, be problems, and these must be faced openly and honestly. But the basic attitude to the Bible need not be discarded. In view of the very great claims that the Bible makes for itself, and that Christ Himself made for the Old Testament, and in view of his own experience of the authority of Scripture, the student who faces some of the problems, or has them thrown at him, should carefully consider whether he can discard the authority of Scripture without creating even greater problems. This, clearly, is a major issue facing those who begin Religious Studies.

AN OPEN HEART

One of the most insidious dangers which arises from Religious Studies is the proverbial familiarity which breeds contempt. 'The subject of the whole Bible is the living God.'[13] But the living God, who has been One to be worshipped and served, becomes an object of cold, academic study, and new information about Him becomes not a guide for living, but material for writing an essay. It requires a conscious effort to avoid this, and a diligence to continue both private prayer and public worship. Ethelbert Stauffer, after a lifetime of studying theology, remarked that 'in temptation theology passes into prayer'.[14] It should be so! Luther put it this way: 'He who studies *mandata Dei* (the commands of God) will not be moved; but he who hears *Deum mandantem* (God commanding)—how can he fail to be terrified?' Similarly Anthony Bloom, in writing about prayer, warns us that 'the realm of God is dangerous'; it is not just for information, but to enter.[15]

Finally, J. A. Bengel, in the preface to the Greek New Testament, 1734, wrote:

'Te totum applica ad textum:
rem totam applica ad te.'

'Apply your whole self to the text: apply the whole matter to yourself.'[16] It is thus, with open mind and open heart, that Religious Studies can be the means for the Christian, like his Lord in the days of His flesh, to 'increase in wisdom and stature, and in favour with God and man'.[17]

Religious Studies

2

The change in name which is taking place in many colleges of education and in some universities, from Divinity, Theology, or Biblical Studies to Religious Studies, is very significant. It reflects both a change of emphasis and a change of attitude. The former names are considered to have too narrow a connotation. They imply a separation of Christianity from other religions, of the Bible from other books, and of the sacred from the secular, or the holy from the unholy. But the notion of secularization, which is becoming increasingly popular (in various senses and forms), removes such distinctions. Religion is life, and life is religion; what is deepest down within a man, or what he feels most strongly, is claimed to be God; so that no man can be an atheist. The strongest objections to this, of course, come from the atheists, who resent being informed that they are really believers all the time. The practical result for Religious Studies is a considerable broadening of the areas covered in study.

The effect of this in the new types of syllabus is that the Bible is less central than it was previously. This is partly the intention and partly the result of the change. In some cases it is the intention, because the Bible is no longer considered to be supremely important and authoritative, and so it is being increasingly displaced; in other cases, the syllabus is broadened to include various forms of modern theology and studies of religion (for example, comparative religion, and the phenomenology, sociology, psychology and philosophy of religion), with the result that the time available for biblical study is drastically reduced.

A SENSE OF DIRECTION

These wider studies do indeed have their value; but the student is liable to get lost in the vast area covered. With the gradual displacing of the Bible to varying degrees, there is the lack of a basis for religious thought. Moreover, it is not possible to understand the significance of modern thought without grasping something of its historical origins and development. Furthermore, there is today the cult of novelty: what is new is equated with what is true, and there is the assumption that the traditional or 'trad' is bad. Such an attitude is, when considered, somewhat absurd; but unfortunately it is too often adopted without being considered.

If one can stand back and look at the theological scene over the centuries, it is really rather presumptuous to assume that most of the thought of godly men for the last 2,000 years has been wrong, and that the truth has dawned largely in the last few years. Indeed, a study of Christian thought over the last 2,000 years shows that many of the modern issues have been faced, and answered, before. For example, the issue behind the current debate concerning 'the Jesus of history' and 'the Christ of faith' is the relationship between the humanity and the divinity of Jesus Christ, which was a central matter of debate in the first three centuries of the Christian era. After all the literary aspects of the present debate, there remains the same theological and philosophical problem, with the same answers.

Again, Tillich seems to have produced new and profound ideas, but when we look we discover they are rooted in the past. For example, we find his idea of 'the power of being' in Anselm, nine centuries earlier.[1]

A study of the history of the church and of Christian doctrine, covering at least the first few centuries, has been a regular part of the old, traditional study of Divinity. It is still of great value, to give understanding and the chance to make reasoned assessments of current ideas. No-one should dare to discuss deeply the doctrine of the Trinity without first studying early Christian discussion of the subject. He may find, after such a study, that his own neat solutions to the problems are not entirely satisfactory, and will enrich his understanding thereby.

To the student the wide range of his studies can be very bewildering. He needs to decide whether he does or does not accept the supreme authority of the Bible. If he does, this is a sure guide through the labyrinths of modern thought—but not a guide that will always give neat and simple answers. This guide is not a substitute for thought; rather it demands very careful thought. That is why Luther said, 'I do not applaud those who take refuge in bragging about the Spirit';[2] for neither the illumination of the Spirit (important though that is) nor the clarity of Scripture removes the need for using our minds. That is why, also, a knowledge of the history of church and doctrine is important.

WORLD RELIGIONS

It is now increasingly common to study other religions, either separately or comparatively. One obvious reason is the presence in our own country of those who practise these religions, and hence the desire and need to understand them. Another reason is that other religions are studied in their own right, as being a part of the experience of mankind.

Various issues are bound to face the student. First, it is obvious that all religions cannot be true, as some are mutually contradictory. To pretend that all are equally true is to exalt toleration above reason. For example, if Christianity says that Jesus is the Son of God, and Islam says that God does not have a son, and that any such statement is a great sin, then both cannot be right. Of course, some modern reinterpretations of Christianity deny that Jesus is (in the real and full sense) the Son of God, and this does diminish the difference somewhat. Nevertheless it is impossible to pretend that the two religions are the same, even with the most gymnastic double-think.

Then the question arises, whether the God of Islam (Allah) is the same as the God of Christianity. Some would insist that they are not the same. But if both religions insist that there is only one God, in that point they agree, and to make a disagreement is pointless. But each religion claims to have its holy book, showing what God is like. The Qur'an and the Bible do not agree in this : their views are different. It appears therefore that the Christian must agree with the Muslim that there is one God; disagree, in part, about His nature, and how He is to be served; and disagree strongly about how He is to be approached, whether through, or not through, a Son.

The Christian who studies Islam may find that the contrasts with Christianity are illuminating, and he may be led to think more deeply about his own beliefs. He should show (and feel) charity and toleration towards Muslims, but that does not mean that he must pretend that he thinks they are equally right. If a Christian accepts the words attributed to Christ, 'No one comes to the Father, but by me',[2] then he cannot accept Islam.

A study of Eastern religions can have a beneficial effect in making a Westerner question his own thinking. In our materialistic civilization, it is obvious that material things exist, but the existence of non-material, or spiritual, realities, is open to question. To the Hindu the opposite is the case. He knows that there is a world of the mind, a spiritual world, but the physical world may be mere illusion. Such a discovery sometimes has the effect of waking a hard-headed, materialistic sixth-former to reconsider his views; and also of arousing the Christian from excessive preoccupation with the things of this world.

It may be disputed whether Buddhism is a religion, in its 'pure' form, as it has no God or gods; it deals solely with this life and the way to live it. As Christianity also deals with this life and the way to live it, it is natural that there should be something in common, and Buddhism may draw our attention to a certain *Christian* practice, namely meditation, which is often forgotten. However, the *content* of meditation for the Buddhist and the Christian will be different.

A study of the different religions of the world may show some similarities, but it also shows great differences. Each may be considered unique in some way. Christianity is unique in its attitude towards history. It does not have myths of timeless events, such as dying and rising gods, but the history of the action of God in this world. It proclaims not merely a code of living, but a dynamic salvation. It offers finally not the nirvana, the non-describable end of the wheel of life, of Buddhism, nor the impersonal union with the divine of Hinduism, nor the materialistic paradise of Islam, but personal everlasting life with God Himself.[4]

SCIENTIFIC STUDIES OF RELIGION

This aspect of religious study is becoming increasingly in vogue. One of its leading exponents, Ninian Smart, tells us that whereas 'the object of Christian theology is to explore, present and apply the Christian faith', the 'scientific' study of religion is 'not concerned with presenting or applying a particular faith, though it is relevant to such a task'.[5] He adds that the study is scientific, as *not* being theological in intent.[6] Rather, it is phenomenological. This means simply that religion is studied as a phenomenon, or something that appears, among men, all over the world. It deals with the religious aspect of human existence. The first stage is plain description, and this is followed by a search for explanations. Concerning theories about the origin of religion, Smart says, 'None of them can as yet be shown to be correct and most of them are virtually certain to be false.'[7]

It may be observed here that this type of study concerns man, and not God: it is anthropology, and not theology. So the biblical claim that God has revealed Himself is not relevant. It is only the human side of religion that is being studied. However, Smart does make the interesting observation that the idea of unrepeatable history, in the Judaeo-Christian revelation, is 'a radical break with archaic, mythic thinking'.[8] We must therefore ask the question whether this scientific study can find a purely human explanation here, or whether it would admit a divine act as an explanation. If God is the living God, we should not expect to be able to fit all His acts into natural categories. That is an issue which must be considered further. But here the limitations of the subject, which appear to be self-imposed, are noted.

Two other branches of this 'scientific' study are the sociology and the psychology of religion. These again deal with the human aspects of religion, the former being concerned with the group and the latter with the individual. Thus the sociology of religion examines, for example, the cohesive effect of a religion within a group.

Some people feel that psychology has disproved religion; but that is far from being the case. The psychology of religion has been a separate study in its own right for many years, and few writers make any such claim. If a man has faith in God, then, for the psychologist, that faith is a fact, which he may study. Whether the basis of that faith is genuine or not, that is, whether God really does exist or not, is not a question for the psychologist as such. He is concerned with what is happening in the mind, and its effect on the whole life. If a psychologist talks about a father-image, this may explain (in part, at any rate) why a belief in God has a particular form, but not why there is a belief at all.

The phenomenon of conversion is of particular interest to psychologists. (Here we refer to religious conversion in the ordinary sense, and not to 'conversion symptoms' in the psychiatric sense.) It is the human features of this experience which they examine, such as the age of converts, their temperaments and background, and so on. They may discover the effects of mass hysteria, or of indoctrination. But they cannot discover an act of God. That, as such, is outside their field.

The last type of study to be considered here is the philosophy of religion. The scope of this has varied down the years. 'The direct concern of the philosophical theologian', says Heywood Thomas,[9] 'is not God, but language about God'. This fits in with the current linguistic philosophy. He adds that 'the subject matter of all philosophical theology is the concept of God'.[10] So, then, this study starts off with Christian beliefs and tries to understand them intellectually. It is not considered to be the function of this study now to produce proofs of the validity of beliefs, though such 'proofs' do have some value in that they show 'something of the metaphysical character of religious belief and the areas of experience where such belief can be said to be grounded'.[11]

The philosophy of religion is wider than philosophical theology, as it embraces any religion, and not just Christianity. In this respect it follows the same pattern as the phenomenology of religion. In fact, the distinctions between the different parts of this study are not rigid; one part leads on to another. First, descriptive information is obtained about religious experience. This is phenomenology. This is examined with respect to groups of people. This is sociology. It is also examined with respect to individuals. This is psychology. Then it is linked with an understanding of the rest of experience in this world. That is philosophy. But philosophy can also start from the Christian faith as in the Bible.

RELIGIOUS EXPERIENCE

It will be seen that the new Religious Studies is not only broader in its scope, but also different in its emphasis, compared with the older Divinity. The stress is changing from a study of the nature, attributes and acts of the living God, to a study of the experience of man. This follows the general emphasis being put on experience now, and the movement is world-wide. There is the vast increase in the use of hallucinatory or stimulant drugs; the turning to transcendental meditation; the quest for special experiences within the Christian religion; and the various movements such as the Jesus People and those who talk about being 'high' on Jesus. Also in education there is very great emphasis on the experience of the child.

Now it is a perfectly valid thing to examine religious experience. Indeed, it is necessary to do so in order to prevent religion from becoming a mere empty ritual. As Joseph Hart wrote :

'True religion's more than notion,
Something must be known and felt.'

It is also necessary to examine religious experience to ensure that it is genuine and not counterfeit. But for the Christian the result can be serious, if the examination is excessive. It can lead to a centring of interest in oneself instead of God. Luther said that the natural man was *in se incurvatus*, turned in upon himself. He needs to be turned towards God. Faith is basically looking towards God, instead of towards oneself. So the constant studying of experience means looking in the wrong direction.

Of course, in this study the student does not look just at his own experience, but at religious experience in general. But the concentration on experience does mean a consequently diminished study of the Bible. This means further that religion is considered in terms of human experience rather than as the product of divine revelation. Furthermore, the human aspect is emphasized even more by the consideration of *any* religious experience, and not just Christian experience. So the Christian student is liable to forget the origin of his own religious experience, formed from a vital relationship with the living God, whom he has known in Christ and through reading the Bible and praying, both privately and publicly; and in forgetting this he is liable to view his fading or faded experience as a relic of his more ignorant past.

It may seem that two opposite dangers have been mentioned : either the cold, academic, intellectual study of the Bible, which allows, or causes, religious experience to perish, as was pointed out at the end of the previous chapter; or the undue stress on religious experience. But in study these two dangers are the same: for a *study* of religious experience is quite different from *having* religious experience. The study, as such, is objective.

In his study, therefore, the student may well take heed of the advice of Alan Richardson: 'It seems to us to matter very little what an "expert" says about God or religious experience, if he has never known God or possessed a religious experience.'[12] We may add that a Christian student is making little progress in his Religious Studies if he ceases to know God and to possess a religious experience.

But not all would agree!

Modern Approaches

3

There is an increasing stress now on being objective. Religious Studies are put on a par with other disciplines to improve their status, and the study is often claimed to be objective. This means in the first place that having a religious belief or a church affiliation is no longer considered to be a necessary qualification for lecturing in the subject; indeed there are lecturers who seem to have no religious beliefs themselves at all, either because they started that way, or because their own studies have diminished or destroyed what beliefs they once held. Some would claim that this does not matter, as it is not a lecturer's job to convince, and moreover that such lecturers can be perfectly good scholars in their subject. Furthermore, it is not assumed that any student has any personal belief, as the subject may be studied in just the same way as Mathematics, History or Science.

But the idea of being objective needs further consideration. The second and very important point is that it implies having no prejudice. So an objective study of an issue signifies a fair examination of the relevant material, leading to a judgment which others would also accept as a result of the same study. But in practice it is not as simple as this. For example, it may require a subjective judgment to decide what material is relevant; and frequently there is just not sufficient material available to make a completely objective judgment possible.

Indeed complete objectivity is an ideal which is very hard to attain. It is to be noted that in science, which is so often held to be a thoroughly objective field of study, the observer is now recognized as being part of the experiment; moreover, the theories, models and paradigms which a scientist accepts are not selected on an entirely objective basis.

T. F. Torrance, writing on *God and Rationality*, remarks: 'It is surprising how many theologians, and not merely the popular sort, still hold the obsolete notion of science as detached, disinterested knowledge.'[1] He adds an acid comment that 'our psychology insists that detachment is not the sign of rationality but of open-mouthed imbecility!'[2] In other words, complete objectivity in the sense of making wholly detached judgments and assessments is in fact a fantasy. It belongs to a bygone age of positivism.

But there is a genuine form of objectivity which again Torrance describes: 'Objective thinking lays itself open to the nature and reality of the object in order to take its shape from the structure of the object and not to impose upon it a structure of its own prescription.'[3] This is an ideal which the student should consider very carefully. It has far-reaching implications, which we shall consider.

There is, of course, one very important principle behind the stress on objectivity: we accept as true what the evidence shows to be true, and not just what we happen to wish to believe. Now this may be very disturbing. We may have our own cherished beliefs which we have held for years; and to discover that they are without foundation would be a fearful thing. Nevertheless, if they are indeed without foundation, it is better that we should discover this, and acquire the right beliefs.

MODERN SCHOLARSHIP

But this is a great oversimplification; and it is here that the student is liable to find himself in difficulties. It is an unfortunate fact that some lecturers tell students that 'modern scholarship shows that you can no longer believe in such and such'—mentioning various beliefs which the student may hold. Now this is most unfair, and is far from being objective, or scholarly. Modern scholarship has shown no such thing. There is no such unanimity in modern scholarship. The fact of the matter is that modern scholarship has examined and called into question every part of Christian belief and, whatever the particular beliefs in question (here we are referring to those beliefs which have been considered 'orthodox' by Christians in general throughout the centuries), there will be found some modern scholars who now reject them; but other scholars, with equal competence and learning, do not find that such rejection is necessary.

An example of this is the resurrection of Christ. Some claim that it was a purely 'spiritual' resurrection, that is, that the disciples felt that somehow His spirit was still with them and His presence seemed so real that it was just as if He were in fact with them, though His body never came to life again, but just rotted in the tomb.[4] Others, however, claim that the resurrection, in its fullest sense, is the most well-attested fact in the whole of history.[5]

It is clear that these two opposite conclusions cannot both be the result of simple objective judgment. Moreover, it is not sufficient to claim that one's own conclusion is honest, and that the other is not. Impugning character is no argument. It is most important to remember that there are many people who are honest to God, and to themselves, and to true scholarship, who reach conclusions quite different from those of the author of *Honest to God*. The ultimate question is the starting-point of the consideration of the evidence.

MAKING ASSUMPTIONS

This example of the resurrection of Christ involves many major issues, and can therefore be a useful subject for further examination. If we start off by assuming that there is no such thing as the supernatural, and that God does not intervene in this world in any way which is contrary to the laws of nature but that He always and only acts in accordance with those laws, then it follows that Christ did not physically rise from the dead. However strong the evidence may be, it will have to be explained in some other way. Now it must be noticed that those who argue from that presupposition exclude the very possibility of proof. The line of argument is perfectly sound (or at any rate can be) once the presupposition is accepted.

On the other hand, if we start off by assuming, not that a supernatural event did take place, but that such a thing is possible, then the evidence that it did take place is extremely great. Again, the line of argument is, or can be, perfectly sound.

The point has been made clearly by J. V. Langmead Casserley, who, as a theologian, strongly criticized some trends in modern theology: 'If ... some narrow and cramping philosophy has closed our minds to the possibility of the Resurrection then we could not receive the testimony though it were a thousand times more cogent and consistent than it already is. Probably at no point in the whole range of historical and literary criticism and research is the priority of philosophy over history, of suppressed presupposition over conscious thought and conclusion, more evident than here.'[6] This writer is not just blindly and uncritically accepting a traditional belief; indeed, he considers that the Resurrection narratives in the New Testament 'are to some extent confused and even self-contradictory'.[7] What concerns him is that some scholars 'attempt to account for the early and widespread belief in the Resurrection by imagining a situation which is completely contrary to all that the surviving records suggest. . . . All the evidence indicates quite clearly that it was the experience of the Resurrection which created the faith of the apostles—something which intercourse with the human Jesus had entirely failed to do, then as now—and not the faith of the apostles which created the experience of the Resurrection.... Why then does ... a scientific historian and biblical critic take refuge in such wild flights of imagination and fancy? The answer is clear. Because he approaches the historical problem of whether the Resurrection really happened with his mind already closed by the conviction that the Resurrection could not possibly have happened.'[8]

Similarly Alan Richardson, in *The Bible in the Age of Science,* writes: 'The presupposition which the investigator brings to his "scientific" study of the Bible determines what he will find there.'[9] The question of the resurrection is one specific example. The same principle applies to the whole of the Bible. For Bultmann, who has had such a profound influence on modern theology, it was an assumption taken over from the last century that miracles do not happen, and a presupposition that the Gospels are not historical.[10] His whole approach to the Bible derived from this. If we do not share his presuppositions, it is unlikely that we shall find his conclusions acceptable. But part of the problem here is just that there are 'assumptions' and 'presuppositions', which are not directly stated, but are taken for granted.

The same type of issue arises at a further stage in scholarly work. Various statements are made concerning the nature of the biblical literature, or of the early church, and the danger is that 'by constant reiteration certain affirmations come to be treated almost like anxioms', as Stephen Neill has pointed out.[11] He therefore goes on to advise us that 'nothing is more important than that every axiom should constantly be put to the test and verified in every possible way'.

This illustrates one of the biggest problems for the student. So often, both in books and in lectures, certain very great and very important assumptions are made. They are assumed, and not explicitly stated. If the presupposition is stated, and alternative presuppositions are also considered, then the student can consider whether to accept it or not. But the difficulty lies in the fact that he is not aware that there are such presuppositions.

A further aspect of the problem is the type of presentation of modern scholarship which the student receives. He may be directed to only a part of it, and that part may not command the widest assent of scholars. So T. F. Torrance, after giving a survey and critique of the so-called new theology, comments that 'concentration upon the more outrageous stuff that appears on the outer edges of Christian thought can give a false impression of what has been happening in the steady progress of scientific theology'.[12]

We may look at another type of assumption. In a recent book called *The Way of Transcendence*, bearing the sub-title 'Christian Faith Without Belief in God', Alistair Kee states categorically, 'There is no direct experience of God, only experiences which are interpreted in a religious manner.'[13] Then later he states, 'Religious experience means the religious interpretation of experience.'[14] The sub-title may surprise the Christian student; it may appear to be a contradiction. The rest of the book confirms that suspicion; for his whole case is found to rest on the unproved assertions just quoted. This particular example is important, as in the realm of Religious Education today the same assumption seems to be basic : there is no special experience which is religious, but this is just a way of interpreting ordinary experience. Here we are concerned simply to see that this is an assumption, and in fact an assumption which is in flat contradiction to the constant claims of the Bible and of Christians throughout the centuries. The student must decide which assumptions he will make—and why.

AVOIDING ASSUMPTIONS

Perhaps it may seem, from the foregoing considerations, that the best thing would be to make no assumptions at all. That is just what Bultmann considered trying to do, as he explained in his article, 'Is exegesis without presuppositions possible?'[15] What in fact he did accomplish was the removal of former presuppositions; but in the process, he replaced them with his own. He removed presuppositions about divine interference: 'The whole historical process is a closed unity.... This closedness means that the continuum of historical happenings cannot be rent by the interference of supernatural, transcendent powers and that therefore there is no "miracle" in this sense of the word.' His own presupposition, then, was that there was no divine interference.

Seth Erlandsson has written on 'Is there ever Biblical Research without Presuppositions?'[16] He explains that the claim is sometimes made that there are no presuppositions, that is, of faith. It follows from this that the Bible has to be considered just like any other human literature, and explained entirely in this-worldly factors. Thus there is the 'assumption that God did not act any differently in Bible times from the way He does today'; and this implies that 'God acts as though there were no God'. So again it becomes apparent that the presuppositions have not been eliminated, but just changed. In fact they are changed from biblical presuppositions to non-biblical ones.

So we may gather that we cannot avoid making assumptions; but at least we can make ourselves aware of what our assumptions are. Bultmann tried to get rid of the assumptions of the Bible. We can see that Bultmann himself was influenced by the assumptions of his own time (or rather, perhaps, of a preceding generation). 'What we really do need', van Unnik reminds us, 'is ... a severe criticism of our own unexamined presuppositions.'[17]

In his autobiography, C. S. Lewis tells us of discussions with a friend. 'He made short work of what I have called my "chronological snobbery", the uncritical acceptance of the intellectual climate common to our own age and the assumption that whatever has gone out of date is on that account discredited. You must find why it went out of date. Was it ever refuted (and if so by whom, where, and how conclusively) or did it merely die away as fashions do? If the latter, this tells us nothing about its truth or falsehood.'[18] This example of one who was a real scholar and a courageous Christian is worthy of careful consideration. It does take courage to go against the 'intellectual climate', or to challenge it; but this may be necessary.

A BIBLICAL ASSUMPTION

Finally we must consider what presuppositions the Bible itself makes, and whether these are acceptable to us today. There is ultimately one great presupposition, and that is the living God. His existence is never proved, but is assumed from the beginning to the end. But He is not merely a God who exists: He is the living God. The story of the Old Testament is the 'development of the relationship between the living God ... and that empirical people whom God has chosen to become His instrument. . . . The Old Testament gives us no description of God. It tells us nothing of what God is like in Himself. It tells us only of what God is like as He meets with, confronts, and thus reveals Himself to, His people, Israel, in the actions of His Spirit.'[19]

The assumption of the whole Bible is this living God, who speaks and acts, and who enters into fellowship with man. It is the living God who constantly takes the initiative. It is He who made the world and man; and when man turned against Him it was He who took the initiative in restoring that fellowship. It is the living God who controls the forces of nature and human history. 'The reality of God for Israel', writes Pannenberg, 'is not exhausted by His being the origin of the world, that is, of normal, ever self-repeating process and events. Therefore this God can break into the course of His creation and initiate new events in it in an unpredictable way. The certainty that God again and again performs new acts, that He is a "living God", forms the basis for Israel's understanding of reality as a linear history moving towards a goal.'[20]

So history is not just what happens, but what the living God does. Sin is not just breaking laws, but breaking a relationship with the living God.[21] Restoration is not just repentance, but the giving of new life.[22]

In surveying the history of the interpretation of the Bible, R. M. Grant comments: 'There is a unity [in the Bible] which is based upon a fundamental presupposition: God lives and works in history; He has chosen a people to be His own; He has guided, and still guides, the course of this people's life and work, in spite of its rebellion against Him. Without acknowledgment of this presupposition, at least as a "working hypothesis", biblical interpretation is impossible.'[23]

This, then, is the presupposition of the Bible: the living God. To accept Him, as the living God, is to accept a certain view of both nature and history. We must decide whether it is still possible today to accept Him.

We cannot prove the existence of God, nor can we prove that He is the living God. In philosophy, fundamental presuppositions cannot be proved, or they would cease to be fundamental presuppositions. They can only be tested; and the test is that a self-coherent system of philosophy can be built upon them. If this can be done, then all that is shown is that these presuppositions *may* be valid. In the Bible there is presented a whole view of nature and history, with the living God controlling, acting and speaking. It is here maintained that nothing less than this is the irreducible minimum for a truly contemporary and a truly Christian world-view. Without belief in the living God, with all that that belief involves (something of which will be seen in this book) life, history and this world have no real meaning. It is only if God is the living God that truly personal fellowship with Him is possible; and prayer is neither a form of magic nor a psychological exercise, but the expression of such a living relationship.

To accept the living God is an act of faith. It involves not only the mind, by which we formulate our philosophy of life and our understanding of God's self-revelation, but the commitment of the whole of our being to Him. For He is not only living: He is God.

Points of View

4

It has already been pointed out that there are widely differing points of view in Religious Studies and in particular in Biblical Studies, which are the chief subject for consideration here. No one view can make an exclusive claim to scholarship or honesty—at least, not justly. It is therefore particularly unfortunate that in some places the possible validity of various views is not seriously considered : one view, or, at any rate, views from one school of thought, are expounded, and other views, if mentioned at all, are done so in such a perfunctory manner as to imply that they are not thought worthy of serious consideration.

It is for this reason that Leon Morris, in writing a scholary volume of *Studies in the Fourth Gospel,* finds it necessary, as a conservative evangelical, to add a preface as an apologia. He shows from his experience that if he is 'silent about the works of more radical critics, he finds himself accused of obscurantism. If, on the other hand, he decides to take notice of what others have been writing, and to quote them, he may find himself accused of citing authors who do not really agree with his essential position.'[1] Further, because of prejudice against the conservative evangelical on the ground that he 'is a slave of his presuppositions', and 'he is bound to reach certain conclusions', he has to ask the reader to take the book seriously and deal with the argument on its merits.[2] It is pitiful that in the world of scholarship there should be such prejudice; but there is.

It is dangerous to use such words as 'liberal', 'radical', 'conservative' or 'fundamentalist', since they are so inaccurate and are not infrequently used in a derogatory manner. Indeed, Thielicke remarks that the terms 'modern' and 'conservative' are 'not only inadequate but downright misleading'.[3] Similarly, G. W. Anderson, in his *Critical Introduction to the Old Testament*, considers that 'the use of such terms as "conservative" and "radical" ... can be misleading. The aim of the scholar should be to establish the truth, and not to defend "conservative" or "radical" conclusions.'[4] Moreover, giving a label is no adequate substitute for answering a point of view, though this practice is not uncommon.

LIBERAL

The term 'liberal' means 'free' in the first place, implying free from the bondage of traditional views, and free to follow true scholarship wherever it may lead. This, of course, is an admirable ideal. But the word tends to be associated with a particular mode of theological thinking which rejects miracles and the supernatural, and proceeds on purely natural and humanistic assumptions. It is therefore possible for a person to adopt a 'liberal' point of view, and yet to be the opposite of liberal in practice, by, for example, despising other points of view and condemning them as unscholarly.

RADICAL

'Radical', by its derivation, implies getting to the roots of the matter, or investigating very thoroughly. But again the term tends to be used to apply to the conclusions reached, rather than to the methods used, and to refer to a point of view which has moved greatly from a traditional view. In fact, of course, it is possible, after a radical investigation, to conclude that a traditional view is still justified.

CONSERVATIVE

'Conservative' literally refers to the conservation of the past; but it neither includes conservation of every past idea nor excludes radical investigation. It implies a more cautious acceptance of new ideas, not a rejection of them. But again it can degenerate into an unthinking refusal to question traditional ideas. S. S. Smalley reminds us that 'conservative' is 'a slippery term, and its implication must not be exaggerated. What is conservative for Tübingen might well be radical for Cambridge.'[5]

It can be seen, then, that the true scholar should be liberal in his outlook, radical in his thinking and conservative in his conclusions. This means that he examines the issues as deeply as possible, from all points of view, conserves what is good, and accepts new ideas or theories when there is sufficient evidence. Thus Stephen Neill, in writing on *The Interpretation of the New Testament, 1861–1961*, comments that the 'liberal' and the 'conservative' differ in the results, not the methods, of their study.[6] 'It is remarkable, isn't it,' says Thielicke, 'that the lines have become so firmly fixed that people think everyone is bound to take one side or the other.'[7] This is a salutary reminder. There are not just two opposite points of view: there are all sorts of gradations in between. To accept every latest idea is not (as some fondly imagine) being radical: it is being superficial.

FUNDAMENTALIST

The term 'fundamentalist' has been called a 'refined theological swearword'. It is used with such a wide range of meanings (and often merely in a derogatory manner) that its inclusion in theological debate is unhelpful. Originally the word was used of those who held to the fundamental tenets of the historic Christian faith, and a series of twelve small books, called *The Fundamentals* and dealing with these different doctrines, was published in America at the beginning of this century. The authors of the various articles were scholars of repute. But now in theological circles the term tends to be used to imply an unwillingness to think, and the adoption of a closed mind towards all modern scholarship. This may be true of some who are called fundamentalists, but not of all. Alan Richardson equates fundamentalism with 'the traditional view, the theory of verbal inspiration', and by this he means 'that the whole Bible had been written down by the human writers at the dictation of the Holy Spirit'.[8] The issues raised by this will be considered later. But at this point all that need be said is that the theory of verbal inspiration is not necessarily the theory of dictation by the Holy Spirit.

CONSERVATIVE EVANGELICAL

'Conservative evangelical' is a term used by those who hold to the fundamentals of the historic Christian faith without closing their eyes to the need for scholarly study of the Bible and theology by modern methods; they claim, however, that true scholarship does not compel them to abandon their 'conservative' beliefs. In support of this, it may be pointed out that in recent years there has developed a considerable wing of conservative biblical scholarship alongside the radical wing, and it is no longer possible to dismiss conservatism as having no scholarly support. Moreover there are eminent scholars (such as Cullmann, Moule and Pannenberg) who, though not 'conservative', have felt compelled to reach more conservative conclusions.

LITERALIST

'Literalist' is now replacing 'fundamentalist' as a term of mild abuse. It is frequently said of certain sorts of people that 'they take all the Bible literally'. Those who use the term thus claim (of course) that they themselves are much more enlightened, and that they can see that the miracles, for example, are not to be taken literally. But this issue needs more than a jibe to settle it.

First, no-one ever did take all the Bible literally. The Psalmist said that the mountains skipped like rams, and the hills like lambs. Who ever took that literally? Another Psalm invites the floods to clap their hands and the hills to sing. Again, the prophet anticipates that the trees will clap their hands.[9] Does the 'literalist' really believe that floods and trees have hands? Further, the 'literalist' does not take the parables literally. Clearly it is not a case of taking all or none of the Bible literally. It is a serious problem of exegesis (the proper interpretation of the text) to decide what is to be taken literally and what is not. This is, of course, no new problem. It is one with which Origen wrestled in the third century.[10]

One further point must be made : to take a passage of Scripture as literally true does not prevent the reader from gaining a meaning from it also. Some seem to think that these are alternatives. They are not. For example, to take the dividing of the waters of the Red Sea at the Exodus 'literally', that is, to assume that that is what really happened, does not prevent one from seeing this as an act of God with very great significance. Indeed, if it did not really happen, it is difficult to see what significance it can really have : it would only be a parable. It needed more than a parable to convince the Israelites that the living God had chosen them and delivered them!

CONCLUDING THOUGHTS

So, then, the student needs to be aware that there are different views and approaches in Biblical Studies, and that they are worthy of consideration. Whatever the student's own point of view, he needs to consider and understand others. The same needs to be said about lecturers. It is regrettable that some refuse to consider other views seriously. To consider other views does not necessarily imply to change one's own view : it does mean understanding other people and also understanding why one thinks as one does.

It is not uncommon to find lecturers considering it their duty to 'open up' those students whom they consider to have 'narrow' (implying conservative) views, and to make them read and consider more radical views. That is good. But such lecturers do not seem to consider it is their duty to introduce 'radical' students to 'conservative' literature. Perhaps the reason is that half a century ago there was very little literature which was both scholarly and conservative. Now, however, there is plenty, though some close their eyes to the fact.

It may seem confusing that there are such different points of view. To understand this, the student needs to examine both the presuppositions of the scholars concerned, as was indicated in the last chapter, and the general attitude of these scholars, as indicated in this chapter. But after that, it is necessary to read books and hear lectures from the different points of view, and to weigh up carefully the arguments adduced, and then to decide what to accept and what to reject. But to do this, some other matters of major importance also need to be examined.

Miracles & the Supernatural

5

One of the major issues on which there are conflicting views today is the question of miracles and the supernatural. It is of fundamental importance in modern theology, and so much so that conclusions on this radically affect the scholar's approach to everything else; and not only the scholar's, for it concerns every Christian, whether he claims to be a scholar or not. The ultimate question is the nature of the living God and of His relationship with this world.

One preliminary point needs to be made clear: it is quite impossible to simplify the issue and pretend that 'radicals' reject the miraculous and 'conservatives' accept it. There is a great cleavage of opinion, but it is not like this. While it may be true that those who style themselves 'radicals' may in general reject the miraculous, except in a very limited sense, those who accept the reality and historicity of miracles and the supernatural are by no means confined to the ranks of those who may be called 'conservatives'.[1] (But of course in the eyes of some the very acceptance of the miraculous makes a man 'conservative'.)

It is not easy to define 'miracle' and 'supernatural'. Much modern discussion depends on the ideas of the philosopher, David Hume (1711–1776); he defines a miracle as a violation of the laws of nature. Seeing that the evidence for the laws of nature is extremely great (in fact, practically all of our experience), the evidence against miracles happen-

ing is almost complete. Thus he defines miracles in such a
way that there virtually cannot be any evidence for them.[2]

In the same way, we can define 'supernatural' only when
we know what 'natural' is;[3] and it is easy to assume a
definition of 'natural' which simply rules out the possibility of the 'supernatural'. Rather than attempt precise
definitions, we shall try to understand the concepts involved.

THE BIBLICAL PICTURE

The distinction between the natural and the supernatural
in the Bible is not nearly as clear as is often assumed. The
two are both ascribed to God. The God of the Bible is the
living God who created the world and all that is in it, and
who retains control. He is the Lord of the forces of nature
and He is the Lord of history. This is the consistent picture.
So in Psalm 135 the writer attributes to God both the
ordinary things like winds and clouds and the extraordinary
things connected with the Exodus. Events which we tend to
call miracles are regularly simply ascribed to God without
the term 'miracle' being used. As He is the living God, He
is constantly active in the world.

So it will be seen that it is unbiblical to speak of 'divine
interventions', as this implies that in general the world is
just going on by itself, and that now and again God inter-
venes and does something. Rather, the biblical view is that
God is always acting, and so we should speak more correctly
of His usual and His unusual activities.

Nevertheless, the idea of 'interventions' is not entirely
wrong, though the biblical term is 'visitations'.[4] The
implication of this is that, though God is always acting,
there are some occasions on which He acts in particularly
significant ways, either in mercy or in judgment, or a
combination of both. 'We need to recover the sense of the
living God, the God of the Red Sea and of Sinai, the Lord
of history, Who visits the earth with power', as Alan
Richardson reminds us.[5]

So the biblical approach to miracles and the supernatural
is not to put them into a separate category, as distinct from

nature, but to put nature into the same category, namely, the acts of God. So, with Pannenberg, we see 'natural laws as specific expressions of the faithfulness of God'.[6]

'Modern science does not believe that the course of nature can be interrupted or, so to speak, perforated, by supernatural powers.' 'The same is true of the modern study of history, which does not take into account any intervention of God. . . .' 'Modern men take it for granted that the course of nature and of history, like their own inner life and their practical life, is nowhere interrupted by the intervention of supernatural powers.' 'For modern man the mythological conception of the world, the conceptions of eschatology, of redeemer and of redemption, are over and done with.' So says Bultmann.[7] He immediately adds: 'Is it possible to expect that we shall make a sacrifice of understanding, *sacrificium intellectus,* in order to accept what we cannot sincerely consider true—merely because such conceptions are suggested by the Bible?' Käsemann echoes the same words, suggesting that the Jesus of the Gospels, with the 'miraculous aura' of 'supernaturalism', can be accepted 'only by means of the *sacrificium intellectus.'*[8] R. H. Fuller, writing on *Interpreting the Miracles,* follows his mentors: 'Modern man is prepared to accept the healings of Jesus as due to his power of suggestion: the nature miracles . . . he can only dismiss as pious legend'; anyone who believes *all* the biblical miracles 'demands a sacrifice of the intellect'. He then adds (quite arbitrarily, and not without some intellectual snobbery): 'Doctors and scientists who are fundamentalist Christians—and there are many of them— have made precisely this sacrifice, with the result that their professional and religious lives have become completely departmentalized.'[9] We note that he dismisses miracles in the name of science, and then dismisses scientists who disagree, assuming that all who accept the miracles are fundamentalists, and that none of them has thought his beliefs through. This is an extraordinarily authoritarian approach.

So we find that 'modern man' cannot accept the miracles because of 'modern science'. What then must our attitude be to the biblical miracles? One possibility is to treat them as sheer nonsense, and therefore ignore them. Another is to rationalize them. This, in effect, is what Fuller does, in the book just quoted. If a miracle can be explained in purely natural terms (as for example the healing miracles, which are ascribed to suggestion), it is accepted, because it is not really a miracle. Fuller considers that some other 'miracles' will in time be capable of explanation, with the further progress of science.[10] So these are acceptable. The 'nature miracles', however, are dismissed. Thus Fuller does not accept any genuine 'miracles'. Nevertheless he does not totally reject the 'nature miracles', but, faithfully following Bultmann, finds a value in the stories.

MYTHS

Bultmann considers that the miracle stories fitted in with the world-view of the New Testament writers, but not with our world-view. 'It is mere wishful thinking to suppose that the ancient world-view of the Bible can be renewed', he says.[11] He does not therefore simply reject the miracle stories, but interprets them. As every interpreter of the Bible has his presuppositions, Bultmann declares his own : his interest is in what the Bible says for our actual present.[12] This gives the clue to his thinking : his real interest is in the present, not in the past. (We must add that a further presupposition of Bultmann, and his greatest, is existentialist philosophy, as expounded by Heidegger. This centres interest on man's present existence and the understanding of it.) So what really matters for Bultmann is the significance of the miracles for our understanding of ourselves. He does not find much history in the New Testament—because he does not look for it. He considers that the miracle stories are 'myths'.

The use of this term can be very confusing, as it can

bear such different senses. Sometimes it means 'old wives' tales', stories which are not considered to be true at all. But this is not the sense of the term in Bultmann, or in modern theology in general. Myth, as Macquarrie explains, is 'a way of thinking in which the other-worldly and divine are represented as this-worldly and human'; but there is a second usage by Bultmann, as when it is said that the flat earth is a myth, and so here myth is 'primitive science or primitive world-view' which is 'not acceptable or intelligible to the modern mind'.[13] These two uses are mixed up together, and because it is assumed that we cannot accept the second type of myth, it is assumed that we cannot accept the first. So for example Bultmann insists that the resurrection of Christ is 'a completely mythical event'.[14]

DEMYTHOLOGIZING

If the miracle stories are myths, then the only way to understand them is to 'demythologize' them. This word means to 'un-myth' them, that is, to see what is the essential truth behind the mythological exterior. Thus, 'the resurrection of Jesus, demythologized, becomes a creative insight into the death of Jesus as bringing man to the end of himself and of his own resources, and so to a new kind of life'.[15] Now it may appear that Bultmann has entirely removed God from the picture, and that all that is left is a symbolic story which enables man now to live a different sort of life. But this is not in fact the case; because 'Bultmann insists upon speaking of God's decisive act in Christ'.[16] Thus the process of demythologizing is incomplete. The general idea of demythologizing is to remove the historicity, that is, to say that the events did not actually occur; but nevertheless there is still some slight element of history and of God's action, and this is simply that there was a Jesus of Nazareth and that God acted in Him.

An example will show the difference between the ordinary interpretation and application of Scripture, and demythologizing.[17] The story in the Gospels of Jesus stilling the storm may be taken as historically true, and then a lesson might be drawn from it, showing that in just the same way Christ can still the troubled heart, in life and in death. So the power of Christ seen in the physical realm is an illustration (and perhaps proof) of His power in the spiritual realm. In this case, the living God is seen acting in this world in His Son. But when the story is demythologized, the historical reference is denied, and the story is solely an illustration about life now.

If we were to demythologize just one story, that would not make much difference; our faith in Christ would be unchanged. But, as Macquarrie points out in *The Scope of Demythologizing*, 'there is to be no selection. Along with the nature miracles go the healing miracles, and along with them the eschatological teaching, the birth stories and the resurrection stories, so far as any objective reference is concerned. Negation moves into the field of doctrine. "What primitive mythology it is", says Bultmann, "that a divine being should become incarnate, and atone for the sins of men through his own blood!" '[18]

That is what demythologizing really means. We are left with a philosophy of the possibility of authentic existence. That may not be entirely fair to Bultmann, however, as he does not entirely eliminate God. Nevertheless the change from the biblical picture is quite enormous. Instead of the living God taking the initiative in acting in this world, visiting and redeeming His people,[19] both in decisive historical events in the past and still in the hearts and lives of those who turn to Him, and also in the affairs of this world, and instead of the power of the Holy Spirit working in man, we are told that we can understand the possibilities of our existence. What is given to man, according to the demythologized Gospel, is the understanding, through the encounter with God in Christ. It appears that God gives no more than the possibility. Bultmann does speak of 'a transcendent God present and active in history',[20] but he does so in terms of human existence.

There is something inconsistent in Bultmann's position, namely, the fact that his demythologizing is incomplete.

So his followers have tended to move away from his position, either to a more conservative or to a more radical position. Among the latter are the 'death-of-God' theologians. They assert that, in differing senses of the word, God is 'dead'. Perhaps the very existence of such theologians is a sad comment on the dead state of much of the church today; for in a church where the living God is worshipped and known, to speak of His 'death' is nothing less than absurd, however clever the argument. This movement may be the logical completion of Bultmann's work; it may also be a direct result of it. After all, if all of God's acts are demythologized, God is left as a cipher and His removal is easy.

A recent example of such an approach is that of Alistair Kee, who considers that Bultmann is 'a rather conservative Lutheran'! Kee thinks that a Christian need not believe in God just because Jesus did; for Jesus such a belief was indeed central, but this was just part of His world-view; as we have to reject His general world-view, we should also reject His belief in God. So Kee tells us that for man today the 'stumbling block is God'.[21] The only real problem with this is the fact that the result is called Christianity.

SHOULD WE DEMYTHOLOGIZE?

We might have our personal preferences for or against Bultmann's demythologizing; but the real question which we must face is not whether we like the results, but whether this is a correct interpretation of the Bible.

It is possible to demythologize only myths, and this approach to the Bible begins by assuming that what is recorded in the form of historical narrative is in fact myth. We have already discussed assumptions, and have seen what Bultmann's own assumptions are. He treats the miracles (and more) as myth first because by his own assumptions they *could* not have happened, and secondly because he is not really interested in history. But this simply begs the question.

Have we good reason to treat these narratives as myths?

C. S. Lewis has made some important comments: how well qualified is the biblical scholar to detect myths? If a man has spent many years making a minute study of the text of the New Testament and of other people's studies of it, but is lacking in wide reading in and understanding of literature in general, he is 'very likely to miss the obvious things' about it.[22] The way to understand what myth is, is to read lots of myths. It is therefore very significant that Lewis, who was very well versed in mythology, should be so scathing about those who treat much of the Bible as myth. The fact that Lewis himself was not (professionally) a theologian does not disqualify him here; his qualifications for making these judgments were his own vast literary knowledge.

The whole of Bultmann's approach to history is very much open to question. History in the Bible is not incidental, but central. As Adolf Köberle put it: 'The history of salvation that is directly linked to the name of Jesus is fundamentally different from the world of myth. By its very nature myth is without historical context; it describes events of nature that occur and recur in cycles.'[23] All through the Bible God is depicted as acting directly in this world, in the history of salvation. So to remove the history and treat it as myth is not to interpret, but to change the 'essential content.'[24] 'The biblical language about God's mighty acts in history certainly needs interpreting;' says Alan Richardson 'but it does not need demythologizing, because it is not a myth.'[25] Elsewhere the same writer says: 'Those who accept the testimony of the apostles that the resurrection of Christ from the dead was a real event in real history would be wise to reject entirely the use of the words "myth" and "mythological" in connection with the New Testament and its theology.... The Gospel story is utterly different in character from those legendary tales about the gods, the personified forces of nature, which are properly described as mythological, since these do not concern real people or events which can be made the object of historical investigation.'[26]

We have seen that Bultmann's demythologizing is put forth in answer to the needs of 'modern man' and because of 'modern science'. Now to ignore modern man and modern science would be obscurantist; but to capitulate entirely to what it is assumed modern man can accept is equally undesirable. Something more moderate is needed.

The criticisms of John Macquarrie are worthy of consideration, particularly as Bultmann himself wrote a preface to the book which contains them, and acknowledged their fairness. Bultmann had said : 'We cannot use electric light and wireless, or claim modern medical and clinical treatment in cases of illness, and at the same time believe in the New Testament world of spirit and miracle.' Macquarrie's comment is simply that in fact people do just that! He adds that Bultmann's own world-view is out of date : 'He is still obsessed with the pseudo-scientific view of a universe that was popular half a century ago, and anything which does not fit into that tacitly assumed world picture is, in his view, not acceptable to the modern mind and assigned to the realm of myth.'[27]

Now we need to consider whether we can make 'modern man' the basis of our interpretation of the Bible. Certainly we need to try to make the gospel intelligible as far as we can. 'But it is no duty of the theologian to accommodate Christian teaching to the modern secularized self-understanding, and indeed he cannot do this', as Macquarrie reminds us.[28] This is no new problem. In the first century Paul tried to be 'all things to all men'[29] in order to make the gospel intelligible; but at the same time he recognized that, as his message was Christ crucified, this was 'a stumbling-block to Jews and folly to Gentiles'.[30] Again, in his discourse at Athens, Paul took pains to make his message intelligible by linking it with the ideas of his hearers, but he did not thereby compromise it, modify it or change it, though it directly opposed some of their ideas. He would not demythologize the gospel to suit the 'modern men' of Athens.[31]

If we feel that the gospel is unacceptable to modern man, we should do well to consider the words of Herbert Butterfield, writing on *Christianity and History* : 'If we think that these Christian beliefs are out of keeping with the twentieth century, there is good ground for saying that they must have been almost equally anomalous in the Roman Empire of the early centuries of the Christian era, which itself in any case represented a high degree of civilization. ... I am not sure about the existence of any modern obstruction to religious belief which, when we come to the essential point, does not resolve itself into a fundamental difficulty of which the world was already cognisant two or three thousand years ago. Neither the difficulties nor the options before us are as modern as many people think.'[32]

So we find that, though the motive for demythologizing may be good in its attempt to bring out the essential message of the gospel for modern man, it fails in just that, because it is the essential message which is unacceptable to modern man, now as always, and not just the form in which it has been presented. Moreover, in demythologizing the essential message has been changed : the theme of the whole Bible is the living God, and the gospel is His salvation in Christ; but Bultmann's God is not the living God.

MIRACLES, SCIENCE AND HISTORY

We have seen that it is because of 'modern science' that Bultmann deems demythologizing to be necessary. But what is 'modern science'? We must ask whether it is physics, or chemistry, or biology, or some other part of science that has shown miracles to be impossible. We must also ask which scientists they are who say this; and then we must ask whether they are speaking *as* scientists, or whether they are simply speculating as philosophers. For we observe that the claim that science disproves miracles tends to come from theologians rather than from scientists. There are in fact many scientists who do accept miracles as really occurring, and so to say, as Fuller does,[33] that these are all fundamentalists who have made a sacrifice of the intellect, and that they have kept their science and their religion entirely apart, is a ludicrous distortion of the facts, simply showing Fuller's own prejudice. Today there is no such thing as 'science', except in junior schools. There is a scientific method, and there are the separate branches of study, such as physics, chemistry, *etc.*; and so a vague appeal to 'science' is out of place.

The notion of 'modern science' held by Bultmann is, as has already been said,[84] out of date. The different branches of science investigate different aspects of the world and the universe in which we live. They do not deal with everything. Science deals with regular, repeatable events; but history deals with unique events. This means that when we are concerned with a miracle story, we do not ask (scientifically) whether this event always occurs in these circumstances, but (historically) whether this event occurred on this particular occasion. In other words, whether a miracle occurred on a certain occasion is a question for the historian and not for the scientist. Science, by its nature, cannot disprove miracles. The idea that it can springs from the old-fashioned view of the laws of nature as being absolute and unbreakable. In any case, a 'law' in science must be distinguished from a law of the land; the laws of nature are descriptions of what *does* happen, and not what *must* happen; though they may tell us what does not happen, they do not tell us what cannot happen.

Some of the older ideas of science, such as the simple logic of cause and effect, are now found to be inadequate. Thus Waismann says that if logic is right quantum theory must be wrong.[85] The older dogmatic type of science has now gone. This has its relevance for the question of miracles. So, dealing with *The Bible in the Age of Science*, Alan Richardson says: 'In the twentieth century there is a developing recognition that the question whether the New Testament miracles happened is one that can be settled only by historical enquiry, not by the dogmatic assertions of pre-quantum theory physics.'[86]

Science cannot be called in to prove miracles either. For,

as Polanyi has pointed out, 'to the extent to which any event can be established in the terms of natural science, it belongs to the natural order of things.... It is illogical to attempt the proof of the supernatural by natural tests, for these can only establish the natural aspects of an event and can never represent it as supernatural.'[37] Thus if science were to show that a particular miracle could occur, it would at the same time show that the event was not a miracle.

If we are concerned with the resurrection of Christ, we are dealing with one particular event. We are not asking a scientific question about whether men normally rise from the dead, but a historical question about whether on one particular occasion a unique event occurred, namely Christ's resurrection. 'The judgment about whether an event, however unfamiliar, has happened or not is in the final analysis a matter for the historian and cannot be prejudged by the knowledge of natural science.'[38]

Now here lies the problem for the historian. If an event which is reported is very unfamiliar, will he be willing to accept that it occurred? The historian has no direct access to the events themselves, but by examining the evidence he has to try to decide what the events were. As Richardson says, 'Historical method does not rule out that possibility of an event's having taken place because it does not fit into a system of generalizations; it decides that an event has *probably* taken place because the assumption that it has done so makes better sense of the evidence.'[39]

This is something of the modern theory of history. But in practice historical study has often been governed by a particular outlook. For example, Troeltsch, whose writings at the beginning of this century were so influential, said : 'Modern thought, it is held, has proved irrefutably the thoroughgoing continuity of the causal process and has made the dogmatic supernaturalism of the church impossible.... We are left, therefore, with the idealistic-evolutionary theory as the only one that calls for serious critical consideration. In itself this theory is an attempt to rule out every means of isolating Christianity from the rest of history on the basis of miracle, and it is an attempt to present in a purely historical way the validity and significance of the Christian religion. . . .'[40] Elsewhere he states that the historical method rests on the 'application of analogy', and this includes 'the fundamental homogeneity of all historical events'.[41]

The result of the application of this method is plain. With the assumptions of analogy and homogeneity, the historian says that all events, past and present, are of the same sort, and so we understand the past as being like the present. Thus if we do not experience miracles in the present, we do not admit that there were any in the past. They are ruled out by the assumptions and not by the evidence. Once again we see the importance of presuppositions. Here the historian has in fact ruled out miracles on scientific grounds, which we have already said is not permissible.

Theoretically the historian should be open to the evidence, whatever that may be, and he should accept the occurrence of any event if the evidence demands it. But this is an ideal which is hard to attain, and a secular historian states, with remarkable candour, what may in fact happen: 'When the historian is confronted by testimony to the occurrence of a specific event, of a kind which he is profoundly convinced cannot possibly occur, he always says that the witnesses, whether two or two hundred, are self-deceived.'[42]

It is not surprising therefore that the historical evidence for miracles and the supernatural is sometimes held to be inadequate. For unless the mind is at least genuinely willing to accept the possibility that such events occurred, no amount of historical evidence will be sufficient to convince.

There is also a possible theological presupposition against the supernatural. Thus in a book review W. R. Hindmarsh complains that the author 'does not take sufficiently seriously the autonomy which God Himself has given to the created order. This autonomy cannot be interrupted by God without destroying the fundamental character of creation itself'.[43] But how can the Christian find out 'the fundamental character of creation' and about its 'autonomy'? Hindmarsh evidently rejects the biblical view of the living God who is active in His creation, and instead has the God of Deism. His view of creation is in fact derived from the outmoded science, which we have mentioned before. Moreover, the concept of autonomy, whether of the individual or of creation, is fundamentally humanist rather than Christian.

This survey of the question of miracles and the supernatural is intended as no more than an introduction. The student who wishes to think for himself should read some of the books to which reference has been made. At least it should be clear that no-one can justly claim that modern scholarship, or modern theology, or modern science, or the modern study of history has ruled out miracles or the supernatural. We have left it as an open historical question, and for those whose minds are not fixed in advance against certain conclusions, the historical evidence for the reality of the supernatural, that is, the free activity of the living God in this world, is very great. The supreme issue is the reality of the resurrection of Jesus Christ from the dead. If this is historically true, then every other miracle in the Bible can be considered in the light of it. Moreover, one single supernatural event would destroy the whole of Bultmann's case. We must therefore give some consideration to the resurrection.

The Resurrection of Christ

6

'If Christ has not been raised, your faith is futile and you are still in your sins.'[1] That is plain enough! The resurrection is the very essence of Christianity and, from all the evidence we have, this was so from the beginning. Indeed, if there had been no resurrection there would have been no Christianity.

But in theology today all the problems and issues which we have considered so far seem to make themselves felt in connection with the resurrection of Christ. The first question, which has already been mentioned, is whether it was physical or spiritual. Here we must observe, with Stephen Neill, that 'the distinction between a physical and a spiritual resurrection would have been unintelligible to the people of that time'.[2] Resurrection is not the same thing as the immortality of the soul. The Greeks believed in the latter, but scoffed at the former,[3] because to them the body, belonging to this world, would be discarded when the soul was freed from it at death. But in both the Old and the New Testaments the concept of resurrection means a raising of the body, though not necessarily in the same form. Indeed Paul argues strongly for both the resurrection of the body (for the Christian) and its transformation.[4] 'Flesh and blood cannot inherit the kingdom of God'; therefore there must be a spiritual body. He is not arguing for a spiritual survival, but for a resurrection of the physical body, which in the process is transformed into a spiritual body.[5] The general picture of Christ's resurrection in the New Testament (whether we wish to accept it or not) is similarly a physical resurrection; this is indicated by the empty tomb and the physical descriptions, as for example when Thomas is invited to touch Him;[6] but also a transformation, so that the risen body does not have physical limitations, but can be present despite closed doors.[7] 'It is historical and semantic nonsense to speak of resurrection unless a physical miracle is referred to.'[8]

It is sometimes said that the resuscitation of a corpse can do no-one any good, implying that the mere fact of Jesus' body coming to life again has no religious value. However, Christian belief sees more in it than that. It is not that 'Jesus rose', but that 'God raised Him'; that is, the resurrection is always viewed as an act of God. Moreover, it is not a mere act of God in the past: Paul's argument, to which reference has already been made, is that *we* shall live again because *He* lived again. But further, this is not only something for the future: God's power as seen in the resurrection is available for the Christian in his life now.[9] Here we see an historical event together with its significance.

Now for a long time some theologians have been drawing a distinction between two German words for 'historical': *historisch* refers to the event that merely happened, and *geschichtlich* to the event that has significance. The distinction seems to go back to Martin Kähler in 1896.[10] Bultmann makes the distinction very great. We have already seen that his dominant interest is the significance of the 'event' of Jesus for man today. So great is this interest that he loses interest in the event itself. History in itself is unimportant to him, and he does not believe in the resurrection of Christ as something that actually happened. But he does believe in the Risen One. Now while it is true that it is the significance of an event for us that really matters, it is difficult to see how there can be any significance unless there really was an event.

A slightly different version of this distinction between event and meaning is made by J. A. T. Robinson. He

considers that to believe that Jesus rose physically is to
'confuse the categories'; there are two descriptions, in 'man'
language and in 'God' language. According to the former,
Jesus died, remained dead, and His body may yet be found;
but according to the latter, God raised Him from the dead.
Robinson's comment is: 'If it seems necessary to rend the
seamless robe of history, something must be wrong.'[11] This
is rhetoric, and not argument. It is *assumed* that there is no
supernatural to 'rend' history; but this is precisely the question. What in fact are the two categories which are confused
in believing in a physical resurrection? They are not to be
found in the Bible, nor in the events themselves: they
originate in the head of Dr Robinson. The train of thought
can be followed easily: as in *Honest to God*, he rejects a
god 'up there' or 'out there', and thinks of God as the
ground of being; the existence of everything and the whole
of nature depend on God; but 'God' is defined in such a way
as to rule out the possibility of any unusual act such as
might be called a miracle or supernatural. For him, the
supernatural is just one way of interpreting the natural, and
it is nothing separate. Now because of this he interprets the
resurrection spiritually; and this means that, historically,
Jesus did not rise again.

Again we are faced with the problem of history and interpretation. Either we accept the living God of the Bible and find
that the resurrection of Jesus Christ, as something that really
happened, fits into the picture; or we replace the living God by
the ground of being and thereby rule out the possibility of the
resurrection really happening.

THE RESURRECTION AND HISTORY

After Bultmann and his devaluation of history, some of his
followers and successors have gradually found more and
more of history in the Gospels. But the resurrection has
remained a problem, for various reasons. Bornkamm states:
'The events of Christ's resurrection from the dead, his life
and his eternal reign, are things removed from historical
scholarship. History cannot ascertain and establish conclu-

sively the facts about them as it can with other events of the
past. The last historical fact available to it is the Easter faith
of the first disciples.'[12] He strongly denies that 'the message of
Jesus' resurrection is only a product of the believing community'. 'It is an event *in* this time and this world' ... but
'it cannot be observed and demonstrated like any other
event in time and space'.[13]

The problem is whether historical scholarship can deal
with a supernatural event. Perhaps Bornkamm has increased
the problem for himself by the way he states it. *No* event of
the past is directly accessible to historical scholarship; an
event can only be inferred from the evidence available. In
this respect the resurrection is like other events : it has to be
deduced from the evidence of witnesses. If 'it cannot be
observed', nor can *any* past event; but it *can* be 'demonstrated like any other event', in the same way, and indeed
perhaps to a greater degree than most past events.

Also Künneth finds the historicity of the resurrection
'problematical' : for if the resurrection is within history,
then it is relative and not absolute; it 'stands in continuity
with a multitude of other known and unknown factors
belonging to this world'.[14] He explains the problem in regard-
ing the resurrection as an historical fact : 'When the resurrection message is looked at in its essential character it does not
exhaust itself in history but points decisively beyond the
sphere of history.'[15] His conclusion is : 'There are certainly
notable relations between the resurrection of Jesus and
history, but ... the concept of "historicality" cannot grasp
the essence of the resurrection witness, which points rather
to something that transcends history.'[16]

Now the point which Künneth makes here is very important : he cannot either write off the resurrection as 'supra-
history', which is beyond investigation and reason, or explain
it entirely in terms of this world. In one sense it is indeed in
history, in that there were witnesses of the empty tomb
and of the risen Christ; but in another sense it is beyond
history, in that it is an act of God. It is beyond history
only in the sense that the *cause* of the event is not to

be found in this world. So we can say that it is God acting in history.

THE RESURRECTION AND PROOF

Another trend in modern thinking concerns the nature of faith. The issues stand out clearly in Heinz Zahrnt's book, *The Historical Jesus,* which surveys some of the results of modern scholarship. While he criticizes Bultmann for rejecting history because of his theological presuppositions,[17] he thinks that Bultmann, in rejecting historical vindication, preserves the Reformation principle of 'by faith alone'; and in this respect 'Bultmann is more in the right than the newly-awakened orthodoxy'.[18] Then, in discussing the resurrection, Zahrnt says : 'Faith carries within itself its own certainty and needs no miracle to confirm it.' The believer 'is asked not to support his faith on impermissible assurances, *i.e.,* on what is "visible", but to see that it rests on the "invisible" and thereby remains faith. He must always be ready for all false supports to be knocked away by historical criticism.'[19] 'Any wish to provide historical proof of it would be contradictory to the intention of all the New Testament witnesses.'[20] Christians 'do not even believe in the accounts of the resurrection, but in the Risen One'.[21]

This total separation of faith and reason is very unsatisfactory. It is radically different from the biblical concept of faith. In the Old Testament the Israelites are urged to 'remember all the way which the Lord your God has led you',[22] and the recollection of what God has done in the past is the basis for faith in God in the present. The Ten Commandments were given as indicating man's obligation resulting from God's deliverance : 'I am the Lord your God, who brought you out of the land of Egypt, out of the house of bondage. You shall have no other gods before me....';[23] faith and obedience depend on knowing what the living God has done. Zahrnt's 'faith' is more of the nature of credulity.[24]

We must ask what would happen to faith if 'all false supports' were to be 'knocked away by historical criticism'.

Many students are in fact in exactly this position. Modern
scholarship is sometimes presented to them in such a way
as to imply that it is now quite impossible to believe certain
tenets of the Christian faith, such as the resurrection.[25]
But we need to distinguish carefully between saying that
'supports' are removed (that is, for example, that the resurrection *cannot be proved*) and that scholarship has, for
example, *disproved* the resurrection. The latter is simply not
true; the former is the issue. To advocate a faith without
supports is to make a flight into irrationalism.

The distinction between faith in the resurrection stories
and faith in the Risen One is plausible at first sight, but
inadequate. Certainly faith rests in a person and not in a bit
of history. But faith in the Risen One means faith in the
One who has risen, and that involves historical fact. If it
is not historical fact that He rose, then He is not the Risen
One. Conversely, we may ask whether it is possible for a
man really to believe in the resurrection stories without, as
a result, believing in the Risen One.

Perhaps we may find a certain validity in Zahrnt's distinction if we look separately at the beginning and the continu-
ance of faith. The beginning of faith in Christ as the Risen
One follows from learning 'stories' about the life, death and
resurrection of Jesus Christ, and the significance of these
stories; faith in the stories is followed by faith in the
person, and this means the establishment and development
of a personal relationship between the believer and Christ.
The stories do not cease to be relevant, as knowing more
about Him is one way of knowing Him better, though this
knowledge of Him develops by personal communion. As in
the purely human sphere, knowing a person and knowing
about a person develop together : personal knowledge still
has a factual content.

A development of the concept of faith described by Zahrnt
is found in Tillich. He says that 'faith ... has no special
content. It is simply faith, undirected, absolute. It is
undefinable. ... Absolute faith ... has been deprived by
doubt of any concrete content, which nevertheless is faith.'[26]

This is the last stage of the movement from biblical faith to irrationality, and it is the direct result of refusing to let faith be tied to history. The history of the acts of the living God is both the basis of faith and the safeguard of its rationality.

The New Testament call to faith in the Risen One is, despite Zahrnt, linked with evidence, witness and historical vindication. The apostles who first proclaimed the gospel of the Risen One were themselves witnesses, and indeed the basic qualification of an apostle was that he was a witness to the resurrection.[27] Paul made a strong appeal to the evidence.[28]

It is strange that Zahrnt should dislike historical vindication; for he himself quotes with approval the conclusion of von Campenhausen that 1 Corinthians 15 fulfils 'all the requirements of historical reliability which in the circumstances can be demanded of a text of this sort'.[29] He also quotes with approval the words of Ebeling : 'The resurrection directs us not to some nebulous and distant mythical realm, but to a sharply circumscribed place in history.'[30]

It is the theologians, and not the historians, who try to remove the resurrection from the sphere of history. It is noteworthy that von Campenhausen is an historian, and that he is most emphatic that the resurrection 'cannot in any circumstances be withdrawn from the testing of historical investigation'. He also argues strongly for the historicity of the empty tomb, as against the commonly held theory that this was a late 'legend'.[31] The important point of this evidence is that though the empty tomb does not prove the resurrection, if the body of Jesus had been found, that would have completely disproved the resurrection.

We may sum up the situation in the words of Pannenberg : 'As long as historiography does not begin dogmatically with a narrow concept of reality according to which "dead men do not rise", it is not clear why historiography should not in principle be able to speak about Jesus' resurrection as the explanation that is best established of such events as the disciples' experiences of the appearances and the discovery of the empty tomb.'[32]

THE RESURRECTION AND THE LIVING GOD

The historical investigation of the resurrection points as strongly as any evidence can to the reality of the event; but it leaves something unexplained. The stumbling-block of the resurrection consists in the fact that it is an event without analogy. It seems to break through the ordinary laws of history. But this is no reason for rejecting it, unless we prejudge that all events must be of the same kind.[33]

'Men who have been dead and buried for three days do not rise again from the dead and behave as the risen Jesus is alleged to have behaved. This fact was well known before the rise of the modern scientific world-view. . . . It has never at any time been possible to fit the resurrection of Jesus into any world-view except a world-view of which it is the basis. . . . One believes the resurrection on the basis of the historical evidence. . . . But can one really believe that Jesus rose from the dead?' So writes Lesslie Newbigin in *Honest Religion for Secular Man*.[34] His answer is : 'No—not if your starting-point is somewhere else.'

If we start off, as we said above,[35] by assuming that there is no supernatural and that God does not intervene, then no amount of evidence will convince us that Christ did rise; we shall have to try to explain the evidence in some other way. A satisfactory explanation will have to be found for the empty tomb, the appearances, the origin and existence of the Christian church, the change in the holy day from the seventh to the first day of the week, and the change in the apostles themselves. But no other satisfactory explanation has been made yet.[36]

'The weakness of the existentialist theology', as Alan Richardson says, 'is that it has given no rationally convincing account of the origin of the church and its faith on the assumption that the resurrection of Christ was not an historical event.'[37]

But if we start off by making the biblical assumption of the living God, we find that the evidence that Christ rose is fully convincing. We shall not then say that a resurrection is impossible, but we shall ask what kind of world this is in which such an act of God has taken place. We shall be open to admit the possibility of other special acts of God, both in the past and in the present. Our whole understanding of the nature of God and of the person of Christ will be affected by our attitude to the resurrection of Christ; and the reality of our Christian life and experience will follow from that, in fellowship with the living Lord.

Biblical Criticism

7

The Bible, to some, is such a sacred book that any criticism of it is considered to be evil. Now this idea arises from a misunderstanding: criticism simply means using our critical faculties, or thinking. We must use our critical faculties if we are to attempt to understand the Bible at all. Criticism does not necessarily mean finding fault: it means examination. So there can be nothing wrong in criticism as such. Indeed, if we believe that God created our minds, we must use them, as we have already said.[1] Further, a Christian has no need to be afraid of the truth: if his beliefs are true, then thorough investigation cannot harm them, since all truth, however discovered, and in whatever sphere, will fit together.

Such a statement, by itself, is rather naive. But it is the essential basis of any thought and research. There will arise apparent contradictions, and these will need to be resolved; but such resolution is not always easy, or even possible. In the face of apparent contradictions, we need to be careful. First we need to establish that the opposing ideas have a sound basis, and are not just speculation. Then we need to establish that the ideas are correctly propounded, as so often fact and theory are mixed up together. Thus careful procedure can often remove the difficulties. If two opposing ideas seem to have equal foundation, it is better to suspend judgment than to reject some 'truth'. It may be that with further light, the problem will be resolved; if not, then to reject some 'truth' for the sake of making a neat system of thought is unjustifiable. This is becoming evident in some branches of science.

If the student finds some contradictions between, on the one hand, his beliefs concerning the nature and acts of the living God, and concerning the nature and value of the Bible and, on the other hand, the theories put forth under the name of 'Biblical Criticism', it is not wise to reject either without careful consideration. There are some who see the contradiction and simply reject biblical criticism as being evil. But the student who has chosen to do Religious Studies cannot do that; in all branches of study the student has to know and examine points of view which he does not accept, and Religious Studies is no exception. But at the opposite end of the spectrum there are those who, in the light of biblical criticism, reject the inspiration and authority of the Bible in any real sense. This in fact is just as rigid and unscholarly an attitude as that mentioned above.

It must not be imagined that there are here simply two opposite points of view, nor that they are irreconcilable. On the subjects of biblical authority and biblical criticism there are very many and very widely differing views. On both subjects the student needs to know the reasons for his own position and attitudes. The assumptions and presuppositions need to be examined, as we have already seen. It is one thing to accept biblical criticism in principle and quite another to accept its conclusions. In any case one cannot rightly speak of its 'conclusions', as these vary so much from scholar to scholar, and from book to book; and the 'conclusions' which seem most certain at one time are at another time challenged and modified or replaced. Also the details of the methods used in biblical criticism are themselves open to criticism. So it is just not possible to view biblical criticism as something to be accepted or rejected. It must be examined, both in its methods and in its conclusions, and accepted where it is justified. If this seems to be an impossible task for the student, we may compare it with the work of a jury : here the evidence is produced and presented by experts, but the decision on its validity is decided by the ordinary man. The work of the jury is based solely on honesty and common sense. In this way the student should look at the evidence, and decide for himself.

All that is intended here is to survey the area and consider the approach to this part of Religious Studies. The remarks of Pannenberg are worthy of note : 'The believer can only trust that the facticity of the event on which he bases himself will continually be upheld throughout the progress of historical research. The history of critical-historical investigation of the biblical witnesses, especially of the New Testament, by no means gives the appearance of discouraging such confidence.'[2]

TEXTUAL CRITICISM

Now there are various types of biblical criticism which we must look at. The first is textual criticism. The aim of this is to discover by examining the manuscripts (and also ancient translations and quotations) the exact text as it was originally written, and to get rid of the errors which have accidentally crept into the text as it has been copied. An example may indicate what happens. In the Authorized Version of the Bible, the heavenly choir in Luke 2 : 14 said, 'Glory to God in the highest, and on earth peace, good will toward men'; but other translations now say, '... peace to men of good will', or 'among men with whom he is pleased'. The difference is one letter in Greek : either *eudokia* or *eudokias*. The evidence of the manuscripts seems to be overwhelmingly in favour of the latter word, with the 's', which alters the construction of the sentence; and so the later translations are correct.

Another example is in Revelation 1 : 5, where the AV has, 'Unto him that loved us, and washed us from our sins in his own blood'. But more recent translations have 'freed us from our sins by his blood'. Now the reason for the change is not that the translators do not like the idea of being 'washed in the blood of the Lamb', but that the weight of evidence of the manuscripts shows that there is again a difference of one letter : the Greek text should be *lusanti,* and not *lousanti,* and this in English is 'loosed' or 'freed', and not 'washed'.

There are some who decry the work of textual criticism, claiming that the Greek text underlying the AV is the right one, and that the 'improvements' of more recent versions are perversions. But this really shows a fear and ignorance of real scholarship on the matter. It is sometimes said that this 'improvement' of the text has the general tendency to lower the person of Christ. But the facts are otherwise. First, no reputable scholar would produce a text as a result of personal theological prejudice and without the compelling evidence of the manuscripts. If he were to do so, other scholars would show this up for what it was worth. Secondly, the text (or texts, as there is not yet final agreement) does not always lower the person of Christ, but sometimes does the reverse. Thus in the widely-used 'Kilpatrick' Greek New Testament,[8] the reading in John 1 : 18 is not 'the only begotten Son, which is in the bosom of the Father ...', but 'the only begotten God'.

Work is still going on in trying to find the original text, and though very often it seems to be virtually certain what the text should read, there are still problems remaining. There is no infallible method of obtaining the correct text, and personal judgments have to be made on the evidence available. But such judgments are not just random : principles of textual criticism have been, and are being, worked out.

It is important to remember, when considering uncertainties about the text, that the total amount of the text which is uncertain is very small. In the writings which have come down to us from ancient Greece and Rome there are often only half a dozen manuscripts, and sometimes even fewer; but there are at least 5,000 Greek manuscripts which contain all or part of the New Testament. This difference is extremely great. Many of the variants are very small, and what may be said with confidence is that no part of Christian belief hangs in the balance because of textual uncertainty.

With the Old Testament there are different problems, and in some parts the text seems to be rather corrupt.

Another problem is that there seem, sometimes, to be different versions of a book represented by the Hebrew text and
the Greek Septuagint. Much work still remains to be done
here, but again, with a modern translation such as the
Revised Standard Version, we may rely on the text as given
without being led astray.

LINGUISTIC CRITICISM

The original languages of the Bible were Hebrew, Aramaic
and Greek. It may at first appear that translation, though
entailing much hard work, is really quite straightforward.
But to recover the exact meaning of these ancient languages
is a very large task indeed. Thus a word in Hebrew may
occur only once or twice in the whole Old Testament, and its
meaning may not be at all clear. But the same word may
occur in a slightly different form in other related ancient
Semitic languages, and these may give the clue to its meaning. Thus there is a vast area of study in comparing what is
known of these ancient languages. Also in the New Testament
much light can be shed on the meaning of Greek words from
the way they are used in business papyri which have been
discovered. So, for example, Luke 15 : 13 in the AV reads
'gathered all together'; but the newly discovered meaning is
shown in the NEB : 'turned the whole of his share into cash'.
It used to be thought that the Greek of the New Testament
was a special language : to the Classical scholar it was
debased Greek, and to some, 'the language of the Holy
Ghost'. But in fact it is now known to be a language in its
own right, *koine,* or the 'common' language of the ordinary
people. Some time ago, there was a list of 767 words which
appeared in the Greek New Testament and were not known
elsewhere. But discoveries and study of papyri have now
reduced this to fifty, and the number is still decreasing.[4]
Of course, work in this field requires considerable competence in the ancient languages, such as is not likely to be
the possession of the student; nevertheless he should be able
to follow the evidence produced by scholars and gain the

fruits of their labours by reference to good modern commentaries.

The value of these two types of criticism, textual and linguistic, is clear and, though there are differences of scholarly opinion at various points, the student will not find much to worry him here—unless he is subjected to pressure from an extreme type of fundamentalism which looks upon all such scholarly activity as evil, and which insists, in the face of all scholarship, that the Authorized Version with its underlying 'Received Text' is the most accurate. It will be found that fundamentalists of this type reject textual criticism and modern translations based on it (especially the Revised Standard Version) not because of the scholarship, but because they consider that the scholars themselves are wrong in their own beliefs.[5] The reader must decide whether he thinks this reason is adequate.

LITERARY CRITICISM

This type of criticism tries to discover information about how a book was written, when, and by whom. Such criticism is applied to any literature. Thus scholars try to discover whether Shakespeare did in fact write all the plays ascribed to him, or who else wrote them, and what the sources were.

It is this sort of criticism which some feel should not be applied to the Bible, because it is the Word of God and thus stands in a class of its own. If it was written under inspiration from God, then such criticism may seem irreverent. So Vincent Taylor, writing on *The Formation of the Gospel Tradition,* says that 'such a study is foreclosed for those who hold a rigid theory of Inspiration. For them the record comes direct from God; the Gospel is to be received and interpreted, but not to be analysed or traced.' But he adds, 'We gladly recognize the divine element in the Gospels, but we see that they came into existence in human ways.'[6]

Certainly the Bible does make great claims for itself, as the Word of God (and these will be considered later); but it is written in human language and in human literary forms. There is clearly a human as well as a divine aspect of the

Bible, and neither aspect should be ignored. Thus we find history, poetry, letters and Gospels, as different literary forms. Moreover it is clear that the style of writing varies greatly, showing something of the character of the writers. (This is much more obvious in the original languages than in English translations, as the translations tend to even up and smooth out the style, obscuring the differences.) It is this human aspect which can be the object of literary criticism.

In the study of literary criticism, perhaps the most important thing to remember from the beginning is the nature of the art. It is not an exact study where questions can be answered with definitive proof. All conclusions have to be reached by arguing from the evidence, and there is no one simple way of conducting the argument. In fact the most that can ever be obtained is a large degree of probability, and what seems very probable to one may seem very improbable to another. Every conclusion reached is in fact a theory, and this must always be remembered.

Some years ago, C. S. Lewis was asked by the principal of a theological college to read a paper to his students on 'Modern Theology and Biblical Criticism'.[7] He spoke as an outsider, but with considerable experience in literary criticism in non-biblical fields, and his words are worthy of careful reading by every beginner in Religious Studies. As an outsider he had an advantage : 'The minds you daily meet have been conditioned by the same studies and prevalent opinions as your own. That may mislead you.' His conclusion was that so many experts in biblical criticism were not to be trusted as critics : 'they seem to me to lack literary judgment'. One of the examples he gives is Bultmann's comment that in Mark 8 the prediction of the passion is followed by the prediction of the second coming of Christ in an 'unassimilated fashion'. Lewis calls this a 'shocking lack of perception', and after considering the content of the passage in the Gospel, he adds : 'Logically, emotionally, imaginatively, the sequence is perfect. Only a Bultmann could think otherwise.'

This particular example is instructive : Bultmann ruled out the possibility that Jesus could have predicted His passion; he therefore assumes that He did not predict it, and therefore finds that the prediction was pushed into the story without being assimilated. His criticism is governed entirely by his presupposition. But Lewis, not hampered by this negative presupposition, finds perfect harmony in the same story.

There is a further point on which we may consider Lewis's comments. With reference to attempts to reconstruct the origins of the biblical texts, he says: 'This is done with immense erudition and great ingenuity. And at first sight it is very convincing.' But Lewis's personal experiences made him sceptical of these reconstructions. Reviewers had constantly claimed to show 'what public events had directed the author's mind to this or that, what other authors had influenced him, what his over-all intention was', and so on. But in the case of his own books and those written by his friends, Lewis states that in all his experience 'not one of these guesses has on any one point been right; that the method shows a record of 100 per cent failure'.[8]

It would be easy to dismiss this as being irrelevant to biblical criticism. But it is very relevant; for the theories about the sources of biblical books cannot be tested, but where similar theories have been produced in non-biblical fields, and where they have been tested, they have apparently been shown to be false. At least, then, it is necessary to hold these reconstructions lightly, as speculation and not as fact.

Let us look at examples of literary criticism. The introductory remarks of Muilenburg on the book of Ezekiel[9] are illuminating. Until comparatively recently this book (unlike other parts of the Old Testament) 'has been generally held to be a literary unity.... But in more recent times the foregoing position has been subjected to heavy assault by many critics. Instead of a unified work by a single author, there is now presented to us a heterogeneity of materials from different writers and from different times.' Then Muilenburg comments: 'The considerable disagreements in the results achieved by recent scholars does not inspire confidence in their validity. . . . Our conclusion, then, is that the book as a whole comes from him, that while there are expansions here and there throughout the book and perhaps numerous glosses, even these represent essentially the prophet's own point of view.' Here then is a case of literary criticism, after a thorough investigation of other proposed solutions, pointing to the essential unity of the book.

From the headings in the Authorized Version of the Bible it would appear that Paul wrote both the letter to the Hebrews and that to the Romans. Now literary criticism has studied these two cases. The letter to the Hebrews is in fact anonymous, and the evidence (such as that of early references to the letter and of style and content) seems to make it fairly certain that Paul did not write it. But by contrast literary criticism establishes the place of the letter to the Romans in Paul's ministry.

It is not only those of conservative persuasion who look critically at critical methods. Thus G. W. Anderson, in his *Critical Introduction to the Old Testament,* dealing with 'the tools of literary analysis', wrote : 'It may be freely admitted that these tools have often been used unimaginatively and pedantically. Superficial contradictions and unimportant stylistic variations have been used as evidence for the existence of a succession of editors and subsidiary sources. Some critics have required in the ancient writers a standard of consistency and an avoidance of repetition of which they are themselves not always capable.'[10]

So Anderson concludes, towards the end of his book : 'It is impossible to reconstruct in any detail a history of Hebrew literature in the biblical period. There are too many uncertainties of analysis and of chronology. But certain broad lines of development may be discerned.'[11] It is strange that, after this, the writer adds : 'The *fact* ... that the Old Testament is a mutilated literary torso....'[12]

In a similar vein Neill, surveying the progress of New Testament scholarship, has written : 'In theology certain proof or disproof is much less often possible than in the physical or biological sciences. But what hinders progress is the persistence in currency of hypotheses in favour of which

solid and satisfactory evidence has never been adduced';
views tend to be accepted because of an eminent name, or
to be repeated on authority without being tested, and thus a
false certainty arises.[13] In the same way also van Unnik,
introducing *Studies in Luke-Acts,* commented that 'working
hypotheses, by oft repetition, tend to lose their hypothetical
character'.[14]

We have stressed the nature of literary criticism as being
such that its theories cannot be finally proved, but at best
can be shown to be probable. Naturally therefore we wish
to know if there are any external 'controls' which may be
used to test theories, and on what grounds we may consider
theories to be acceptable or unacceptable.

THE CONTRIBUTION OF ARCHAEOLOGY

Archaeology is a discipline in its own right, and there is a
danger in the amateur taking snippets of apparently relevant
information to 'prove' that some part of the Bible is true.
This has been done in the past. But now the subject can be
approached in a much more scholarly way. Essentially
archaeology provides the background, in various respects, for
biblical studies. There is not just the evidence that certain
events really did take place, but also material to illustrate and
illuminate the lives and customs of people in biblical times.
Besides this, there is much known now of the cultural background.

Something of the relevance of this for the literary criticism
of the Bible is vigorously presented by K. A. Kitchen, in his
Ancient Orient and Old Testament. He points out that the
literary criticism began before archaeology flourished, and
claims (with abundant evidence) that some of the theories
which are still widely held today are in fact untenable in
the light of archaeology. 'It is becoming increasingly evident
that—regardless of the date of forms—the literary characteristics of the Ancient Near Eastern treaties make nonsense
of the usual criteria of conventional literary criticism.'[15]

In the first place it appears that the form of the Sinai
covenant (as in Exodus and Deuteronomy) agrees with the

normal pattern in the late second millenium before Christ, the time when it is supposed to have been given; but it is different from the normal form as used in the first millenium when, according to the commonly-held theory of Pentateuchal Documentary Analysis, it was finally written in its present form. This in itself proves nothing about when the account was written, but only supports its accuracy. What is much more significant, however, is that the form of covenant corresponds to that in the *complete* narrative as we have it in our Bibles, but it does *not* correspond with the form in the supposed sources, 'J', 'E', *etc.* 'The explanation is surely that our existing Hebrew text exhibits an original literary form actually used in antiquity.'[16] If we accept the usual literary analysis, we find the incredible situation that the earlier sources had a covenant form which did not correspond with those known from antiquity, but that when they were put together later, the resultant form then agreed with that of the distant past to which the composite document refers.

A further type of argument used in literary analysis is that of 'doublets'. This means that if there are two somewhat similar stories, it is assumed that they are really the same story preserved in parallel strands of tradition. Thus there are two stories of Abraham pretending that his wife was his sister, first in Egypt, and then in Gerar.[17] It is claimed that the former is the version of the 'J' source, and the latter of the 'E' source, and that they both refer to the same incident. But the theory is complicated by the fact that there is another similar story, namely, that of Isaac acting in the same way.[18] This, S. H. Hooke tells us, is 'an altered version of E's story' inserted by 'a later reviser of the J narrative'.[19] Hooke comments: 'Whether such an explanation can be considered wholly satisfactory is a question which cannot be discussed here. It will not satisfy those who are already finding the documentary hypothesis inadequate. But it must be confessed that it is also not easy to find a satisfactory explanation for all these duplicates in the Yahwist's intention of writing . . . salvation history.'[20] It may be naive to suggest a simple solution, that Abraham had a fixed policy in this matter, and that his son followed his example.

In the same commentary H. G. May, writing on Joshua, says: 'The quite complete confusion in OT scholarship in the differentiation between the J and E sources in Joshua examplifies the difficulty in making such a distinction.'[21] So the theory itself does not account for the phenomena which it was invented to explain. But most of the work of scholars is done in making ever more complicated analyses, from the biblical text, and in studying each other's work.

But to get help in assessing the validity of the arguments used, we again turn to archaeology. Kitchen finds some parallels to these doublets, in other ancient texts.[22] There are ancient accounts of two kings, Tuthmosis I and III, going on campaigns to the Euphrates, erecting stelae, and hunting elephants: but no-one would assume that these were duplicate accounts of one set of events.[23] So, then, in biblical narratives we should not assume that similar stories are really two accounts of one story, and are thus evidence of different sources.

The two creation stories in Genesis are similarly held to be from different sources. Again, Kitchen gives several literary parallels from ancient texts, where there is first a general account, and then a detailed account of the same event.[24] In the cases cited, there is no question of there being different sources. Because of this, and also because the two creation stories do fit together as being complementary, the fact that there are two cannot be adduced as evidence of two sources.

But of course there are other arguments used: thus it is claimed that there are different styles of writing in the supposed different sources. In the creation stories, however, any differences are due to the nature of the content. But again, archaeology shows differences of style in one piece of writing, in one inscription.[25] So we find that those features which, in the Bible, are claimed to prove different sources, are seen elsewhere in a single source. This makes the evidence for these sources look very slender.

The work of Professor M. H. Segal of Jerusalem on the Pentateuch should be more widely known.[26] He is severely critical of the now traditional Documentary Theory. 'The Documentary Theory works exclusively with philological and literary tools, and represents a philosophy now antiquated. It ignores completely the rich finds of modern archaeology.... This scepticism of the Theory, as well as its pedantry and artificiality and the absurd lengths to which it carries the analysis of the text, breaking up homogeneous passages, and even single verses, into small fragments for their distribution among its various documents, have met with much just criticism, but the criticism failed to upset the Theory.... The principal assertions of the system, originally nothing more than pure suppositions, have now matured with age and with constant repetition into axiomatic truths, which control the thinking of scholars and direct their approach to biblical problems.... Hebrew literature, or any other literature all the world over, cannot show another example of the production of literary work by such a succession of compilers and redactors centuries apart, all working by one and the same method, as attributed by the Theory to the formation of the Pentateuch. But besides this striking artificiality, the Theory also puts forward highly improbable assumptions without offering any evidence for their veracity.'[27] Segal's own approach is to start with the assumption of a basically Mosaic authorship, for which he finds good reasons from archaeology, and then to decide what parts, for critical reasons, cannot have been written by Moses. (Of course nobody, not even conservatives, accepts that *all* the Pentateuch came from Moses.) We cannot here give the details, but we note the type of critical argument which he finds invalid : 'We would not admit as decisive arguments against Mosaic authorship based upon our modern rationalistic mode of thought which declares passages with miraculous contents to be legendary and therefore of a late origin.... Moses himself could have told the story of the extraordinary events he had experienced as a series of divine miracles for the realization of the great purpose for which he laboured.... Finally we must reject the arguments against the Mosaic authorship of the Pentateuch based upon the modern hypo-thetical reconstruction of the history of the religion of Israel on evolutionary lines. These arguments are simply begging the question. For that reconstruction is itself based upon a denial of the Mosaic authorship of the Pentateuch and of the authenticity of the Pentateuchal record of the story of Israel's religion.'[28]

THE STUDY OF TRADITION

Linked with archaeological study is the so-called traditio-historical method. Notable in Old Testament studies in this field in Ivan Engnell, who considers that criticism has gone astray because it has thought in modern, instead of ancient, terms: 'it is necessary that we free ourselves from the modern, anachronistic book-view and that we view the Old Testament realistically as a product of the ancient Near Eastern culture, of which Israel and its national literature, the Old Testament, are a part'.[29] He adds that, because of archaeology and philology, we need 'completely different perspectives with regard to the text and the tradition.... Newly oriented research in the history of ideas and history of religions had freed itself from the evolutionary doctrin-arianism of an earlier period.'[30]

Here is an essential point on which this type of criticism differs radically from the 'orthodox' literary criticism: the basis of much of the latter was the assumption of a steady evolution of religious ideas, by which it was assumed that 'primitive' ideas revealed that a passage was early, and 'advanced' or 'developed' ideas indicated that a passage was late. This principle, which is a matter of pure speculation, has been used to rewrite the history of Israel's religion. Engnell clearly indicates the different approach: 'A funda-mental principle of the traditio-historical method can be de-duced: *confidence in the tradition,* even where oral tradition is involved. This principle is diametrically-opposed to the view-point of literary criticism, which in reality implies a fundamental censure of the tradition and text.'[31] We must add Engnell's own warning : 'It hardly seems necessary to point out that the traditio-historical method is still in the first stages of its development and that, therefore, in a great many cases, its results must be regarded as preliminary.'[32]

What seems to be important about this approach is that it attempts to take seriously into account the ancient background to the writing of the Old Testament books, and as a result finds much less change and more reliability in the content.

Parallel with Engnell's work on the Old Testament is that of Gerhardsson, another Scandinavian, on the New Testament.[33] In view of the Jewish background of New Testament times, he claims that, far from undergoing a steady development, the tradition of the words of Jesus was learnt from Jesus Himself, and passed on reliably (though he does consider that the early church reshaped the Gospel material). This view is diametrically opposed to the developments of literary criticism in form criticism. How valid Gerhardsson's work is will be seen, as scholarly debate on it continues. But again, it has importance as looking for outside controls in dealing with New Testament material. It acts as a brake on the wilder forms of speculation.

PROPHECY AND CRITICISM

It is often said that in Old Testament times a prophet's job was to proclaim the Word of God to the people, forth-telling rather than fore-telling. There would be a small measure of foretelling, or prediction, concerning the fairly immediate future. Thus a prophet may first warn the people not to disobey God, and then, when they have disobeyed Him, predict punishment. It is regularly assumed that the prophets did not predict the distant future, as this would have no relevance to the people to whom they spoke. But we must consider whether this assumption is correct. The derivation of the Hebrew term for a prophet (nabhi) is uncertain; it may be connected with an Accadian word (nabu) meaning 'to announce'.[34] But the real meaning of the term in Hebrew can be found only from the way it is used. In the Bible, in fact, the prophets do look forward to the distant, as well as the immediate, future. The idea that they did not is based on the rationalistic assumption that there is no supernatural, and that therefore prophets *could* not predict the distant future. If therefore there is, in the writings of a prophet in the Bible, a prediction of the distant future (as it would have been to that prophet), then some critics would ascribe this passage to a later writer, thus making the prophecy either a prediction of the immediate future, or a *vaticinium ex eventu*, a 'prediction' made after the event.

A good example of this is in the book called Isaiah. It is regularly assumed now, and often as being beyond dispute, that there are at least two 'Isaiahs'. The first, Isaiah of Jerusalem, is the one who appears in chapters 1–39. The rest of the book is ascribed to an anonymous prophet of the exile. Or chapters 40–55 are ascribed to this unknown prophet, and the remaining chapters to one or several other writers. The main reason for this division is that the second half of the book deals with a period about one and a half centuries after Isaiah of Jerusalem lived. As there are prophecies in the form of predictions concerning this later period in some detail, it is assumed that the writer must have lived at that time. Now it is not proposed here to attempt to prove whether there were one, two or three Isaiahs. The aim is to see what sort of arguments are used in literary criticism, and whether they are valid.

Here the basis of the argument is the definition of a prophet as one who spoke to the people about their own times only. But this is a circular argument. The definition can be maintained only by removing from the writings of the prophets all predictions of the distant future, and then asserting that they never spoke (or wrote) about the distant future. And the basis of this is that there is no supernatural. A prophet could not, and therefore did not, predict the distant future. So the result of this assumption is the assertion that the person who gave the prophecies about the exile must have lived in the exile.

Certain observations must be made about this. First, the book as it stands is evidence of such prediction. But this particular form of criticism simply removes the evidence. Then it should be noted that the second part of the book of Isaiah stresses that the Lord, the living God, the God of Israel, can predict the future, and that in this He is different from the false gods.[35] Yet it is just this which many critical scholars deny.

There are also supporting arguments connected with the language. But these by themselves are not strong : certain differences in style can be attributed to differences in content, and if the argument is made from the vocabulary, then, because of the large number of words which occur in chapter 40 and not elsewhere in the book, it would appear that that chapter was not written by the author of 'Second Isaiah', though in style and content it fits in perfectly. Thus the argument from language can be made to prove anything, and cannot carry much weight.

Nevertheless, the question still remains, and may be posed in a different form. While belief in the living God takes away the force of the argument that Isaiah of Jerusalem did not, could not or would not speak or write about events of a century and a half later, the question is why he should have uttered such prophecies, and to whom. If, after weighing the evidence and sifting the arguments, the the student decides that Isaiah 40ff. was not written by Isaiah of Jerusalem, but by 'the unknown prophet of the Exile', the value of those chapters will still remain. Whatever the human agency, the product can be recognized as a divine self-revelation.

Another example of this issue connected with prophecy is the book of Daniel. Again, it seems in many quarters to be assumed to be a fact that the book was written in the second century BC, and not in the sixth, which is the setting of the book as it presents itself. Thus in his commentary on the book, Norman W. Porteous assumes this as beyond question, simply reproducing the arguments as stated by

Driver at the end of the last century, and not considering evidence which has come to light since then.[36]

The chief argument for the dating of the book is that, though the setting is the sixth century, the writer in his 'predictions' seems to betray a considerable knowledge of the second century. It is assumed that he could not predict the distant future in such detail, and that therefore the book must have been written in the second century. This theory is then supported by claims that the language (Hebrew, Aramaic and a few Greek words) demands the later date, and that certain historical references to the sixth century are incorrect.

All this may sound very convincing unless the facts are known. The argument about predictions will not carry weight to one who believes in the living God. The arguments from the languages are now seen to be equivocal: the Hebrew and the Aramaic could both have been written in either the sixth or the second century, and the same is possible for the few Greek words. Possible solutions have been found to the historical problems.[37] There is, however, one further point: in the Hebrew Bible, Daniel is not included among the books of the prophets. This may seem to point to the date not being the sixth century. But when all the evidence which can be adduced is put together, it is seen to be not nearly as strong as at first appears. The student must decide for himself about the date, after weighing the evidence; if he finds himself unconvinced by arguments either way he may need to have the courage to keep an open mind. It must again be remembered that the value of the book does not depend entirely on its dating.

We have already noticed how the same issue of prediction has arisen in New Testament studies: Bultmann rejects the possibility of Jesus making predictions about His passion, and so these predictions are assumed to have been made by the early church after the event, and then put back into the story of Jesus' earthly life. But this leads on to another type of criticism.

FORM CRITICISM

This branch of biblical criticism attempts to trace the development of the forms in which units of tradition about the words and deeds of Jesus existed before they were written in the New Testament documents as we have them. We shall consider this method as it is applied to the New Testament, but it has also been used extensively on the Old Testament.

It will be apparent that the method makes a number of large assumptions. These, as pointed out by Redlich,[38] are that there was a period of oral tradition before the Gospels were written; that this tradition was passed on in separate units (except for the passion narrative); that the material may be classified by its literary form; that it was the practical needs of the Christian community which produced or preserved the forms; that there is no chronological or geographical value in the traditions; and that the original forms of the traditions may be found by studying the laws of tradition. And the comment of Guthrie on these is: 'Very few of these assumptions can be considered valid.'[39] This does not mean that form criticism must be rejected, but that its assumptions and developments must be constantly reviewed.

It is not uncommon for the process of handing down this tradition to be compared with the party game in which a statement or brief story is passed round the circle of friends in a whisper and, after it has been passed on perhaps a dozen times, the final version is compared with the first. The result is often very entertaining. But to compare this game and the life of the early church is, when considered, rather absurd, even though the comparison is made by some otherwise worthy scholars. In the game the message is whispered once to each person, and most of the confusion arises because of the physical difficulty of hearing. Moreover this is a game, and is intended to entertain. But in the early church, the message was not an insignificant story, but what was considered to be of supreme importance; it was not whispered, but preached and taught; it was not heard once, but repeatedly. So the comparison is highly misleading.

An illuminating illustration of what really happens in

passing on the Christian message orally can be found in the recent history of the spread of Christianity in New Guinea. The missionary encouraged the native converts to spread the gospel to surrounding areas. They were very careful to get the message exactly right. ' "Wait, now, you listen to me," one of the natives would say. "I want to repeat the story to you. See if I tell it right. I don't want it to be wrong when I go to my village.... Just sit down and listen to me, then you can go back to your work." '[40] Here, then, we find a strong desire to get the story exactly right; this is a far better example to consider than the party game, as the situation is much nearer to that of the early church.

On the first page of his *Essays on New Testament Themes* Käsemann says : 'The work of the Form Critics was designed to show that the message of Jesus as given to us by the Synoptists is, for the most part, not authentic but was minted by the faith of the primitive Christian community in its various stages.'[41] It must be noted that this was *designed* and it must be viewed accordingly. But Käsemann then adds that in present-day criticism 'efforts are being made to show that the Synoptists contain much more authentic tradition than the other side is prepared to allow'.[42] However, he considers that there is only enough history in the Gospels 'to prevent the Christian message from dissolving into a myth';[43] and it is clear that he finds this quite satisfactory. Once again we see how much the criticism is governed by presuppositions.

So often it is said that we only know Jesus through the early church, as He Himself wrote nothing. From this it is argued that we have a distorted view, and that we only have 'the Christ of faith' and cannot reach 'the Jesus of history'. But the trend of scholarship now, though starting from this basic position, is to find more and more genuine information about 'the Jesus of history'. It should be remembered that if we cannot know the Jesus of history direct, the same applies to most figures of ancient history : we know them only from their impact on others.[44]

Form criticism looks, for the origin of the Gospel material, not to Jesus Himself but to the early Christian community. This principle, which is a basic assumption, is open to the gravest doubt. In the first place it is a strange sort of criticism which makes the evidence say the opposite to what it appears to say; this is not to say that criticism is unjustified, but if the evidence seems to say that all the Christian message goes back to Jesus Himself, and that it was this which produced the Christian community, it will need very strong argument to show that the reverse was the case, namely, that the community produced the message. If we have the Christian community, we may argue that it produced a Christian message, but we still have to show what produced the Christian community. It is this that form criticism has failed to do.[45] It is characteristic of individuals, and not communities, to be creative and, as Piper has said, 'it is time to demythologize the myth of a creative community'.[46] It is really very strange to suggest that 'the anonymous community had far greater creative power than Jesus of Nazareth, faith in Whom had called the community into being'.[47] This is what the more extreme form criticism implies, and all form criticism centres attention on the community rather than on Christ in seeking the origin of units of tradition.

But there has been a change of emphasis. Formerly it was the recognized custom in form criticism to look for the *Sitz im Leben* (that is, 'situation in life') in the church to find the origin of traditions; but now it is being recognized that there can also be a *Sitz im Leben* in Jesus Himself. This means that formerly it was assumed that if any unit of tradition fitted into a situation in the early church, then that was the origin of that tradition. This is really a baseless assumption : to show that something *could* be attributed to the church does not mean that it *must* be. So it is being recognized that various units of tradition fit into both the life of the church and the life of Jesus; so they could have originated with Jesus and been preserved by the church. The result of this broader approach is to recognize much more authentic material in the Gospels.

There are other points on which form criticism is very vulnerable, as has been pointed out by many, such as C. F. D. Moule,[48] D. Guthrie,[49] S. C. Neill,[50] G. E. Ladd.[51] First, as Vincent Taylor pointed out many years ago : 'It is on this question of eyewitnesses that form criticism presents a very vulnerable front. If the form-critics are right, the disciples must have been translated to heaven immediately after the Resurrection.'[52] The whole idea of the development of tradition, or of the creation of new tradition, ignores the fact that there were eyewitnesses about up to the time when the Gospels were written. In particular, the role of the apostles is ignored : according to the evidence available, it was the duty of an apostle to bear witness to the teaching and acts of Jesus, and especially the resurrection; not to create or develop, but to preserve.[53] Again, it is said that the early church was not interested in history; but there are indications that it was, as Moule points out.[54] So in fact the early Christians were interested not just in the Risen One, but also in the resurrection.[55] To them the resurrection was 'a unique event set in historical time.'[56] Further, it is assumed that the early church did not distinguish between facts and interpretations, and between Jesus Christ before and after His resurrection, so that a message given by a prophet in the early church (we are told) could be attributed to the earthly Jesus. But the evidence of 1 Corinthians 7 shows a clear distinction between what Jesus on earth said and what was received from Him by the Spirit later. Again, it is assumed that the tradition about Jesus was passed down in units, which may be traced separately; this has not been demonstrated to be true, and the admitted fact that the passion narrative was passed on as a connected, continuous tradition is evidence to the contrary.

For an assessment of form criticism, after this brief survey, we may consider a recent editorial in the *Expository Times* : 'One must confess to a certain disappointment with the total result. ... Their conclusions are so mutually contradictory, and their assessment of the same evidence so diverse . . . The main impression the reader receives is that the investigations are still in their very early stages, and that it will take some time yet before agreed gains can be clearly distinuished from interesting but unconvincing hypotheses.'[57] That is fair, and a healthy corrective to the unwarranted dogmatism sometimes heard or read.

But form criticism has made, as Ladd puts it, 'a substantial contribution to an evangelical understanding of the Gospels in a negative way. Form criticism has failed to discover a purely historical Jesus.'[58] The aim was to demonstrate that Jesus was a purely human, historical figure, and that with the development of tradition He was transformed into the divine Christ. But 'the purely "historical Jesus" is a hypothesis of a modern criticism that derives its presuppositions from modern philosophies, not from the biblical accounts'.[59]

REDACTION CRITICISM

The latest development from form criticism is called redaction criticism. As one of its exponents, Norman Perrin, has written a book called *What is Redaction Criticism?*[60] the student may find here a useful summary of the methods and claims, with various examples. We shall refer with some comments to what Perrin says.

Whereas form criticism deals with units of tradition, readaction criticism investigates how these units were put into complexes and how the Gospels were formed. So redaction criticism assumes and builds on form criticism. It is now assumed that the writers of the Gospels were not merely collectors of materials, but authors, and the aim is to discover the theological motives of these authors.

When the method is applied to Mark's Gospel it is bound to be largely speculation, as there is no means of proving or testing the results. Perrin says: 'We analyse the constituent parts of the narrative, such as the sayings, etc., to see what they tell us of Mark as one who gathers, modifies, or creates tradition. . . .'[61] But we can see how Mark gathers or modifies tradition only if we know what the tradition was before he touched it; and we do not. This is only a subject of critical speculation. It is difficult to see how it could be shown that Mark created, as distinct from used, a tradition, though Perrin tries to do this.[62]

'Mark has the right to be read on his own terms, and after several generations of being read mistakenly, as a historian, he has earned the right to be read as a theologian.'[63] Now it is useful to consider Mark as a theologian, but to put this in opposition to being an historian is quite unnecessary. We have been told for a long time that the Gospels are not biographies; but that does not prove that they contain no biographical material. It may seem quite clear that the Gospels are not intended to be mere biographies or mere histories; but to cut out history altogether, as is popular amongst some scholars, is uncalled for. We must distinguish between history and a chronicle of events or a diary. To group events together according to their subject matter may present a clearer picture of what sort of a person Jesus was, and of what He did, than a diary-type account; and so this would rightly be called accurate history. If therefore Mark sorts his material out to some extent, as a theologian, this does not make him cease to be an historian. Setting the tasks of theologian and historian in opposition is not the result of a study of the material in the Gospel, but a result of the presupposition that history does not matter. If Perrin is not interested in history, that does not prove that Mark was not.

'We must take as our starting point the assumption that the Gospels offer us directly information about the theology of the early church and not about the teaching of the historical Jesus, and that any information we may derive from them about Jesus can only come as a result of the stringent application of very carefully contrived criteria for authenticity.'[64] It must be noticed very carefully that the idea that the Gospels tell us about the theology of the church, and not the history of Jesus and His teaching, is clearly stated here to be an assumption, and a starting-point. Yet a few pages further on, Perrin claims that redaction criticism 'is forcing us to recognize that a Gospel does not portray the history of the ministry of Jesus ... but the history of Christian experience in any and every age'.[65] This is really quite extraordinary: what is first stated to be an assumption and a starting-point is then claimed to be proved, by a flagrant *petitio principii*, begging the question.

There is a further large assumption, which has already been referred to in form criticism: 'The early church, not having our sense of the word "historical" and being motivated by an intense religious experience, saw no reason to distinguish between words originally spoken by Jesus bar Joseph from words ascribed to him in the tradition of the church. In this respect the New Testament is very different from the records we have of Jewish rabbis or Greek teachers in the ancient world.'[66] Two comments must be made: first, the assumption about the early church is quite unwarranted, as we have seen, and as C. F. D. Moule has shown:[67] and second, the assumption that the New Testament is so different from the records of Jewish rabbis is worthy of more than casual mention. Gerhardsson takes this up in detail, and therefore comes to quite different conclusions about the historical reliability of the Gospels.[68]

The work of redaction criticism on Matthew and Luke rests on a surer foundation. With Mark it was necessary to speculate on the tradition before Mark touched it, and so to speculate on what Mark did to it. But as literary comparison of the first three Gospels seems to show fairly certainly that Matthew and Luke used Mark's Gospel, it is possible to see how they used it, and what alterations they made. An example often quoted, from Bornkamm, is the story of the stilling of the storm. Redaction critics tend, like Perrin, to ignore the question of the historicity of the incident, and just examine its theological interest to the writers of the Gospels. Now it may well be that the different writers of the Gospels do bring out different theological emphases; but that raises the question of whether they created these emphases. I. H. Marshall, in considering *Luke: Historian and Theologian*,[69] argues that first, Luke is an historian (still!) as well as a theologian, and secondly, that he found the theology in his sources and thus he retained, and did not create, it.

We see then that, whereas form criticism stressed the theological activity of the Christian community, redaction criticism stresses that of the individual writers. It can have considerable value in drawing attention to the theological significance of even the details of the Gospels.[70] But it disparages history, not by proof, but by assumption.

Perrin's conclusions about the value of form criticism are : 'It will be a decade or so at the very least before the work will have progressed far enough for there to be sufficient agreement among the scholars concerned to provide the basis for a summary of achieved results.'[71] Similarly Moule says : 'It is unfortunately true that, so far, there is not much unanimity about the results.'[72] With such warnings, the student will be careful to keep readaction criticism in perspective.

THE QUESTION OF HISTORY

We have already repeatedly mentioned the question of history and in particular in connection with the resurrection of Christ.[73] Now we must consider it further. Much current theological thought echoes the maxim of Kähler that the real Christ is the preached Christ.[74] So Fuller tells us that Christian faith is in Christ as proclaimed by the church today, so that the role of historical research is subordinate; and the Christian believer need not 'fear because the professors are always changing their minds or disagreeing among themselves'.[75] Perrin like Zahrnt, goes a little further : he considers that faith alone is required, and 'faith as such is necessarily independent of historical facts, even historical facts about Jesus. . . . A faith built upon historical fact would not be faith at all but a work.'[76] But this is not biblical faith : it is existentialism. In the Old Testament there is a constant call to have faith in the living God who is known by what He has both done and said; the Exodus was one such act of God, and if it had not happened there would have been neither the nation nor the religion of Israel. Similarly in the New Testament there is the witness to the resurrection as an event in history. It is this stress on history which distinguishes biblical faith from paganism : 'pagan religions have no sense of history', but in the Bible there is 'the peculiar attention to history and to historical traditions as the primary sphere in which God reveals Himself', as G. E. Wright puts it.[77] He adds : 'Inner revelation is thus concrete and definite, since it is always correlated with an historical act of God.'

We see then that there are two opposite approaches to history : Perrin says that it is unnecessary and Wright says that it is essential. Of course many others follow these divergent lines. Now we cannot simply accept the view that happens to please us : we need a basis for our choice. Perrin, as we have seen, makes his attitude to history his basic assumption in studying the Bible; but Wright argues that his is the biblical attitude.

Now this is significant; for we find that those who reject the New Testament history are not historians, but theologians.[78] So Montgomery comments : 'Historians who stand outside the existentially suffused atmosphere of New Testament study are frequently at a loss to know what is troubling the Christian historian.'[79] On the same issue F. F. Bruce says : 'Whether the task of extracting historical data from the Gospels is impossible or not is for the historian to discover, and not for the theologian to tell him; and one thing that no self-respecting historian will allow himself to be told is that his quest is illegitimate.'[80] So we find that Sherwin-White, writing on 'The historicity of the Gospels and Graeco-Roman historiography', finds it 'astonishing' that Graeco-Roman historians have been increasing in confidence, but that 'study of the Gospel narratives, starting from no less promising material, has taken so gloomy a turn'.[81]

It is a surfeit of existentialism which has turned some New Testament scholars to such an anti-historical mood, as this philosophy's chief concern is with man's understanding of himself and his own existence. But the Bible's chief emphasis is on the living God, and man's relationship with

Him. If therefore we start with the Bible's own presupposition, we find that it is full of history.

Of course, not all modern scholarship has succumbed to the anti-historical mood. To see history in a better perspective the student should study, for example, Richardson,[82] Pannenberg,[83] Moule,[84] and Marshall.[85] The question of history is one of the major issues in theology today, and the tide seems to be turning. Amongst the most radical scholars there is a tendency to find more history in the New Testament now, and less extreme scholars have never abandoned historicity.

Something of the change in Old Testament studies, in this respect, may be seen by comparing the books of Oesterley and Robinson and of Bright.[86] So in the former, for example, written in 1932, we read concerning the patriarchs: 'It will be obvious that narratives which originate as we may guess these to have done will have comparatively little value for the historian.'[87] But in Bright, written in 1960 (and revised in 1972, but unchanged here), we read: 'The patriarchal narratives ... fit precisely in the age of which they purport to tell. ... The essential historicity of the traditions cannot be impeached. ... Enough can be said to make it certain that the patriarchal traditions are firmly anchored in history.'[88] And it is as a result of archaeology and critical study that this change has come about.

We may end this brief survey on history by quoting what G. E. Wright said twenty years ago: 'In some theological quarters one gets the impression that the historical criticism of the Bible has left the faith on such shaky and unprovable historical foundations that we need to find another and firmer basis. ... The so-called destructive nature of biblical criticism has been exaggerated and misrepresented. On the contrary, we today possess a greater confidence in the basic reliability of biblical history, despite all the problems it has presented, than was possible before the historical criticism and archaeological research of the past century, and especially of the past three decades.'[89]

THE UNITY OF THE BIBLE

'Since the dawn of criticism the approach to the New Testament has been largely analytical', says Hunter.[90] The same may be said of the Old. The result of this approach has been to stress the differences and diversity within the Bible, setting in opposition the legal and the prophetic books, the priestly and the prophetic religion, the Gospels and Pauline religion, the Jesus of History and the Christ of faith, the Old Testament and the New Testament, so that, as Rowley reminds us, half a century ago to write of the unity of the Bible 'would have involved some suspicion that the author was an out-of-date obscurantist'.[91]

But the newer approach is synthetic. So in 1943 A. M. Hunter wrote *The Unity of the New Testament*, and in 1953 H. H. Rowley wrote *The Unity of the Bible*. This synthetic approach is not so much the opposite as the complement to the analytical. So in the New Testament, after thorough analysis and the discovery of variety and diversity, we find that the writers 'were using different idioms, different categories of thought, to express their common conviction that the living God had spoken and acted through His Messiah for the salvation of His people'.[92] In a very similar way, G. W. Anderson writes about the Old Testament: 'Together with the variety, there is also a constant: a confession of faith in God's saving acts on behalf of His people.'[93] The nature of this unity is, in Rowley's phrase, dynamic, and not static.[94] So another Old Testament scholar, Knight, comments: 'Even while we observe this growth in faith and understanding on the part of Israel, we become aware of the paradoxical truth, that the thought patterns of Israel hardly changed all throughout the whole length of Israel's history. For example, the wild and primitive poetry of that wild and primitive woman, Deborah (Jud. 5), contains *in essence* much of the faith of the later prophets.'[95] This dynamic unity is seen, then, in the development of living faith in the living God.

It is significant that this new stress on the unity of the Bible comes not just from conservative scholars, but from 'most biblical scholars today'.[96] And what is more significant is the recognition of the cause of this unity. 'The continuing thread that gives unity to the record', says Rowley, 'is the divine element'; for it is found to be not a record of the life and thought of Israel and of the church, but 'a record of Divine revelation'.[97] The student would do well to ponder carefully the words of Alan Richardson : 'The longer we spend in reflection on this subject, the more we are impressed, as we read our Bibles, by the unity of the whole Bible, and the more likely we shall be to revert to the view that the inspiration of the Holy Spirit had probably something to do with the matter after all.'[98]

But that leads to a subject which we shall consider in more detail, in a separate chapter.

CONSERVATIVE TENDENCIES

There has been a tendency for a number of years now on the part of some scholars in favour of more conservative views. Something of this has already been seen, in that greater historical reliability has been accorded to the Old Testament as a result of archaeological research, and an increasing amount of the material of the Gospels is admitted as authentic, by critical scholars. But of course not all scholars share in this tendency, and some of the 'radical' are becoming more radical. Nevertheless in his *Critical Introduction to the Old Testament,* Anderson says that there is some ground for stating 'that there has been a "conservative reaction" in contemporary criticism'.[99] Similarly, in his article 'Current Trends in British New Testament Studies', Smalley states : 'If anything, as we shall see, the drift of scholarship in matters of form as well as theology is continuing to run in a critically conservative, but balanced, direction.'[100]

This tendency towards more conservative views is due, so Rowley tells us, less to new knowledge than to new approaches; the critical method has turned 'against some of the conclusions that had been too easily accepted'; but this new conservatism 'is both other and firmer than the older conservatism, just because it is critically, and not dogmatically based, and because it is built squarely on the evidence'.[101]

The 'older conservatism', which is so disparaged by many scholars, is that which prejudges all issues and refuses to look fairly at modern scholarship. Hence, as we have seen,[102] 'conservative' tends to be a dirty word. It is therefore with some hesitation that conservative conclusions are accepted. So Fuller, writing on the Fourth Gospel, says: 'The discovery of the Dead Sea Scrolls has opened up new possibilities that some of the conservative positions were right after all'; later he says that it is 'quite responsible scholars, and not only those with conservative predictions' [sic! presumably 'predilections'] who are beginning to consider a much earlier date for the Gospel.[103] This distinction between 'quite responsible scholars' and 'those with conservative predilections' is a flagrant example of argument by definition, such as one would not expect from a responsible scholar.

One important feature of the conservative tendencies in Old Testament studies is, as Rowley indicates, 'the treatment of the Old Testament as a fundamentally religious book.... Beyond that it has been emphasized ... that the Old Testament is a book through which Divine revelation of enduring importance to men is given.'[104]

BIBLICAL CRITICISM AND CHRISTIAN FAITH

Finally, if we are prepared to take biblical criticism seriously, we must ask, with Professor Moule: 'Is, then, my faith in Jesus, whom I know as alive and as my Lord, vulnerable to the researches of scholars? Could critical scholarship discover something that might render that faith impossible or null?' It is worthy of note that, although the answer which Moule gives is: 'Theoretically, yes', he nevertheless concludes: 'Those who, through the apostolic witness and in the Christian Church, know Christ as Saviour and Lord, are sufficiently sure of Him now to be convinced that, in fact, such a thing will not happen.'[105]

Disclosure or Discovery?

8

There are basically two different ways of looking at the Bible : as an account of God seeking man, or of man seeking God. The picture given of the nature of God may be viewed as either God's own disclosure or man's own discovery. Of course, as in other matters, a total separation of two opposites is far too great a simplification, but the basic difference must be carefully considered. The real question is whether God or man is to be the centre of our thinking.

In Religious Studies there has been an ever-increasing emphasis on man, man's nature and man's experience. Thus there is a tendency for theology (the study of God) to devolve into anthropology (the study of man). The greatness, glory and transcendence of the living God is somewhat of an affront to the dignity of man, and so instead some speak of God's humility—a remarkable metamorphosis of the biblical doctrine of God's grace. Similarly in Relious Education there has been the tendency to move from talking about God to talking about 'Who am I?'

The biblical perspective is the opposite to the modern tendency. So when Moses asked 'Who am I?', his thoughts were turned instead to consider who God was.[1] Similarly, at the beginning of his career as a prophet, Jeremiah thought of his own abilities as being inadequate, and his

thoughts were turned away from himself to God, who promised him all that he needed. These are not isolated verses,
but this is the whole tenor of Scripture. Indeed this fits
in with the consistent supernaturalism of the Bible, which
we have considered. If we take the Bible at its face value, we
find constantly that it is the living God who is active and
seeking man, and that when man seeks God, this is in response to God's initiative. Many Christians have said as
Augustine did : 'I should not have sought Thee unless Thou
hadst first found me'; for, in looking back over his past
life, a Christian often finds that choices which at the time
seemed to be entirely his own now appear to have been
given by God. It is this double aspect of the human and
the divine which we find in the Bible. The problem is to
keep both in mind, and in the right perspective.

Biblical criticism is, in principle, a study of the human
side of the Bible; but if the human side is viewed in isolation, we may arrive at false conclusions. As we have seen,
where prophecy, for example, is concerned, to view it as
purely human is a denial of the acts of the living God; and
so the divine element needs to be considered in biblical
criticism even when studying the human aspects of the
Bible. The same applies to accounts of miracles : a judgment about the genuineness of miracles affects our literary
judgments about many parts of the Bible. Again, the process of handing on the tradition in connection with either
the Old or the New Testament, is regularly considered in
purely human terms; any possibility of the working of the
Holy Spirit of God in the process is tacitly ignored. But
when the Bible as the finished product is considered (apart
from theories about its composition) a remarkable unity
appears in it, as has already been discussed.[2] So as G. A.
F. Knight says : 'Despite its multifarious origin, the Old
Testament presents us with a unity of thought such as no
human mind could ever have impressed upon it.'[3]

THE INFLUENCE OF SCHLEIERMACHER

In 1799 Schleiermacher published his book, *On Religion:*

Speeches to its Cultured Despisers.[4] Like Bultmann who came more than a century later, he tried to fit Christianity into a modern world-view, and thus to make it acceptable. In the second speech he argued that the practical part of life is the realm of morality; the thoughtful and contemplative part is the realm of science; and so religion is pure feeling.[5] Thus the essence of religion can exist without 'miracle, inspiration, revelation, supernatural intimations'.[6] Now this was a cunning way of meeting opposition to Christianity : it could not be challenged on either its intellectual content or its actions, because these were not its proper sphere; as its proper sphere was feeling, this was above attack.

But this redefinition of Christianity, or, rather, religion, radically altered its nature, and has had a lasting effect. Schleiermacher has been called 'the father of modern theology'. He strongly refused to equate religion with doctrine, as religion was not knowing but feeling. Of course we must agree that religion is not *merely* knowing, and is not *merely* doctrine : but that does not mean that we need to remove knowing and doctrine from religion. Nevertheless this is what has happened. The result has been both a devaluation of history, as we have seen,[7] and a rejection of the whole idea of 'revealed truth'. This means a refusal to accept at their face value biblical claims that God has both acted and spoken.

But for a considerable time now the tide has been turning. While scholars who adhere strongly to existentialism and who insist on interpreting the whole Bible existentially find no need of revelation in the acts of God in history or in communication from God, there has been a widespread tendency to reconsider the whole idea of revelation, and in particular to recognize God as revealing Himself by His mighty acts.

GOD WHO ACTS

Twenty years ago G. E. Wright wrote a book which exemplifies this tendency: *God Who Acts.*[8] He said : 'The primary means by which God communicates with man is by His acts, which are the events of history.'[9] But the classic statement of this approach was made by William Temple in his Gifford Lectures of forty years ago.[10] His persuasive argument and elegant words are often quoted; and he concluded that 'there is no imparting of truth as the intellect apprehends truth, but there is event and appreciation; and in the coincidence of these the revelation consists'.[11] 'There is no such thing as revealed truth. There are truths of revelation, that is to say, propositions which express the results of correct thinking concerning revelation; but they are not themselves directly revealed.'[12] So 'what is offered to man's apprehension in any specific Revelation is not truth concerning God but the living God Himself'.[13]

Now this sounds very attractive and reasonable; and if we have simply the choice which Temple suggests between 'truth concerning God' and 'the living God Himself', no doubt it is the latter which we want. But such an antithesis is quite false. Of all the things that happen in this world, how do we know which are the acts of God? And if we do recognize acts of God, how do we find the living God Himself? So Wright, though he stressed the primacy of God's acts, also said: 'It is obvious that such events need interpretation before their true meaning can be understood. Consequently, when God acted, He also "spoke" in numerous ways, but especially by chosen interpreters.'[14] 'By this means of human agents God provides each event with an accompanying Word of interpretation, so that the latter is an integral part of the former.'[15]

GOD WHO SPEAKS

Now this is one of the greatest issues in the whole of Religious Studies: not only whether God has revealed Himself at all, but whether He has, in any real sense, 'spoken'. One important contribution to the discussion is John Baillie's *The Idea of Revelation in Recent Thought*.[16] He closely follows Temple, considering that 'God does not give us information by communication; He gives us Himself in

communion'.[17] He claims to find 'a remarkable breadth
of agreement in recent discussion' on this.[18] But it is easy
to find agreement by ignoring those who disagree; and he
totally ignores, for example, the writings of Warfield.[19] Despite himself, Baillie finds himself forced to go beyond the
limited recognition of God acting. So he says: 'The
prophets and apostles all believed that only by God's own
aid were they able to interpret His mighty acts.'[20] Later he
remarks very significantly: 'A man cannot embrace Christ's
salvation without assenting to the fact that Christ is such
as to be able to save.'[21] The point is that it is no use at
all simply to know that Christ died; but it is supremely
important to know that 'Christ died for our sins'.[22] Without the interpretation, the event is meaningless.

Now it is instructive to observe what 'modern scholarship' has said on the subject. Baillie claims that he has the
weighty authority of Kittel's *Theological Dictionary of the
New Testament* behind him. There, under the Greek word
apokaluptô, meaning 'reveal', Oepke says: 'Revelation is
not the communication of supranatural knowledge... but
it is quite essentially the *action* of Yahweh.'[23] Baillie's judgment on that dictionary is that it 'is as nearly impartial and
as little tendentious a work of scholarship as is available'.[24]
But James Barr, in a detailed study, comes to quite different
conclusions. He finds that Oepke's article on the Greek word
does not start from the Greek word, but from a 'certain
conception of "Revelation" which is of course a central
notion in much modern theology'; and 'the article is assimilated to modern theological usage', instead of being based
on the biblical usage of the word. So, dealing with the Old
Testament background of 'revelation', Oepke considers that
God revealed Himself through His mighty acts, 'although
there is not a place in the Old Testament where these
"mighty acts" are referred to with g-l-h "reveal"'. Barr
adds that Oepke 'practically neglected' the New Testament usage of the term 'revelation', as in 1 Corinthians 14,
where it refers 'to an individual at a particular time'.[25]

So it appears, then, that the Bible itself does not support

the claim that revelation is just by God's acts, and it appears further that those who try to limit themselves to revelation by God's acts are inevitably led to include interpretation. In the Bible we find that act and interpretation go together. So with God's mighty acts in the Exodus, there was Moses who gave God's interpretation; with the Exile, there was the prophet Ezekiel to explain; and Amos said: 'Surely the Lord God does nothing, without revealing his secret to his servants the prophets'.[26] It must be noted that the biblical claim is that the interpretation comes from God, and not from man. 'Revelation consists in both—in the event as such and in its interpretation', as Cullmann stresses.[27] 'This inclusion of the saving message in the saving events is quite essential for the New Testament.'[28]

We must go a stage further: the Word of God does not only accompany or follow His acts to explain them: it also precedes them. So with the Exodus, God spoke, according to our records, before He acted; and 'this spoken and then acted Word of God, moreover, was virtually a revelation of God's very heart and purpose'.[29]

The significance of God speaking before acting is seen when we look at the relationship between Jesus and the Old Testament. As Pannenberg put it: 'Jesus is the revelation of God only in light of the Old Testament promises.'[30]

THE BIBLE'S CLAIMS

In biblical theology it is normal to consider such subjects as the doctrine of God, of Christ, of man, and of salvation, that is, to consider what the Bible says on these subjects. It is equally important to consider what the Bible says about itself. We have seen a little of what biblical scholars have been saying, and now we must see what the Bible itself claims. The points which have arisen so far have concerned the fact of God revealing Himself at all, His revelation in His acts, and His revelation in 'speaking'; we have not considered the relationship between the revelation of God and the Bible.

THE OLD TESTAMENT'S CLAIMS

The claim that God has spoken is remarkably frequent. The expression, 'Thus saith the Lord' and similar expressions occur, so we are told, well over 3,000 times. To feel the force of this, the reader is recommended to go through the book of Amos (the first of the prophets with a book under his name) and to note every occurrence of these expressions. The claim is not that the prophet had an experience of God, and then put into his own words what he thought he ought to tell the people; rather, the claim is that the prophet felt under a divine compulsion to speak what God said. Amos was not trained to be a prophet and did not want to be one; he spoke only because he had to.[31] This is the normal picture of a prophet.

The same is said of Moses: he is described as being reluctant, but urged on by God Himself: 'Go, and I will be with your mouth and teach you what you shall speak.'[32] So with Balaam we read: 'The Lord put a word in Balaam's mouth, and said. . . .'[33] It will be observed that the claim is that God gave His servants the words to say; that is, both the message and its very form are ascribed to God.[34]

There is also the claim that 'Moses wrote all the words of the Lord'.[35] Such a statement needs to be taken with caution. The first five books of the Bible were traditionally ascribed to Moses. Now it cannot be claimed that the verse quoted must refer to the whole of those five books; but at the very least there is the claim that Moses did write, and that what he wrote was 'all the words of the Lord'. Similarly it is claimed that Joshua wrote what God said.[36] Also, the book of the prophet Isaiah claims both that God spoke to the prophet and that God commanded him to write the message down.[37] Again, the later writings of the Old Testament echo the claims just mentioned, referrring to 'the book of the law of Moses, which the Lord has given to Israel'. [38]

The Old Testament, then, constantly claims that God spoke to His servants; there are claims that some to whom God spoke wrote His words (though the extent of this is not made clear); and much of the Old Testament is in the form of accounts of what God said. Of course, claim is not proof; and here we are concerned to note the claim.

CHRIST AND THE OLD TESTAMENT

The New Testament makes great use of the Old Testament, and we may safely assume, from its frequency and consistency, that this use goes back to Jesus Himself.[39] In the first place, according to the Gospels, Jesus used it in His own life. So when He was tempted, He answered by quoting the Old Testament; He would not act in a way contrary to its teaching.[40] He cleansed the Temple, because of what the Old Testament said about it.[41] He knew that He had to suffer because the Old Testament said so.[42]

Jesus claimed that the Old Testament referred to Him and was fulfilled in Him. So His first recorded word was 'Fulfilled...'.[43] Also in the synagogue at Nazareth, after reading Isaiah 61:1, 2, He claimed that the words were then being fulfilled.[44] Again, according to the Fourth Gospel He claimed that the Scriptures testified of him.[45] According to Luke, Jesus 'beginning with Moses and all the prophets, interpreted to them in all the scriptures the things concerning himself'.[46]

Jesus considered the Old Testament to be from God. When He was talking about divorce, He quoted Genesis 2:23, 24 as being what God said, though in the book of Genesis these words are by the author; thus Jesus counted the text of the Old Testament as being God's Word, even when the words are not there ascribed to God.[47] Again, when Jesus quoted Psalm 110, He said, 'David, inspired by the Holy Spirit, declared...'. That is, Jesus attributed the writing of the Psalm to the inspiration of the Holy Spirit as well as to the work of the human author.[48] In disputing with the Sadducees, Jesus said that they were wrong because they knew 'neither the scriptures nor the power of God', and then He quoted Exodus 3:6 as being what God said.[49] Thus He acknowledged the Old Testament as being *the* source of true knowledge of God and His ways, and the final answer to a religious question.

Jesus acknowledged the supreme authority of the Old Testament. He said that He had come not to abolish, but to fulfil the law and the prophets, and that 'till heaven and earth pass away, not an iota, not a dot, will pass from the law until all is accomplished'.[50] Far from abolishing the law, He saw a deeper meaning in it, and insisted that it should be kept not only in one's actions, but in one's thoughts and motives.[51] Jesus considered the Old Testament to be God's Word through Moses and the prophets in such a way that if anyone did not accept it, he would not be convinced even if someone rose from the dead.[52] That is, He considered the authority of the Old Testament to be abundantly clear, and not needing a miracle to support or prove it.

Jesus constantly alluded to the Old Testament, showing that His mind was filled with it.[53] According to the evidence of the Gospels, Jesus contradicted the beliefs and practices of the Jews of His day in various ways, but He never contradicted their view of the supreme authority of the Old Testament. He claimed to speak and work with God's authority;[54] but He never set this in opposition to the authority of the Old Testament.

CHRIST'S FOLLOWERS AND THE OLD TESTAMENT

So the consistent picture in all the Gospels is that Jesus regarded the Old Testament as the Word of God and as of the highest authority. His example was followed by the apostles, according to the accounts of the speech of Peter (Acts 2) and of Paul (Acts 13). They repeatedly referred back to the Old Testament in their proclamation of Jesus as the Messiah.

The different New Testament writers treat the Old Testament in the same way. Thus the author of Matthew's Gospel himself (as distinct from the sayings of Jesus which he records) keeps on saying: 'This happened that what was spoken might be fulfilled ...'.[55] The author of the Epistle to the Hebrews begins by saying that 'God ... spoke by the prophets'.[56] Also in quoting the Old Testament, he says:

'The Holy Spirit says'.[57] Further, the same writer, in his first chapter, gives seven quotations from the Old Testament, and in each case he ascribes the words to God.

Paul similarly can write: 'The scripture says to Pharaoh . . .',[58] thus evidently equating 'Scripture says' with 'God says'. So again: 'The scripture, foreseeing . . . preached, saying . . .'.[59]

Then 2 Peter 1:21 says, with reference to the Old Testament: 'Men moved by the Holy Spirit spoke from God'; and 2 Timothy 3:16 says; 'All scripture is inspired by God'. This, literally translated, is; 'All scripture is God-breathed'. Now the meaning of this is plainly not that God gave some special value or authority to men's words, but that the words of scripture have come from God Himself—God breathed them out.[60]

G. W. Anderson ends his *Critical Introduction to the Old Testament* with these words: 'The New Testament writers use the Old Testament, not only as the scenery for the drama of salvation, but as the record of earlier acts in that drama. Jesus Himself, Who used the Old Testament Scriptures with sovereign freedom, understood His own work as their decisive fulfilment. His use of them remains the supreme sanction of their place in the Christian Bible.'[61]

In his careful study of *The Authority of the Old Testament*, John Bright comes to this conclusion: 'I am quite unable to get around the fact—though Harnack, for example, said he was not impressed by it—that the Old Testament *was* authoritative Scripture for Jesus Himself. Jesus knew no Scripture save the Old Testament, no God save its God; it was this God whom he addressed as "Father".'[62]

Such, then, is the supreme authority of the Old Testament which it claims for itself, which Jesus Christ acknowledged and which the apostles and New Testament writers likewise accepted. Such a claim cannot be lightly ignored. But before its acceptability is further considered, we must look at the authority of the New Testament.

CHRIST AND THE NEW TESTAMENT

Of course we do not have any account of Jesus' attitude towards the New Testament as we have of His attitude towards the Old, for the obvious reason that it was not written until after His earthly life had ended. Nevertheless some of His words are very relevant. According to the Fourth Gospel He gave the promise of the Comforter : 'The Comforter, the Holy Spirit, whom the Father will send in my name, he will teach you all things, and bring to your remembrance all that I have said to you.'[63] So also : 'When the Spirit of truth comes, he will guide you into all the truth; for he will not speak on his own authority, but whatever he hears he will speak, and he will declare to you the things that are to come. He will glorify me, for he will take what is mine and declare it to you.'[64]

So when we consider the passing on of the tradition of the words and deeds of Jesus, and the writing of the Gospels, we should remember that Jesus promised the aid of the Holy Spirit in this sphere. And when we consider the growth and development of the early church as in Acts, and the writing of the Epistles, we should remember the promise of Jesus that the Holy Spirit would lead into all the truth. And when we consider the Revelation, with its apocalyptic descriptions of the future, we should consider also that Jesus promised that the Holy Spirit would show things to come.

THE NEW TESTAMENT'S CLAIMS

The repeated claim of the New Testament writers is that the Holy Spirit, through whom the Old Testament Word of God came, was still active in giving the Word of God in the Gospel of Jesus Christ. Thus in 1 Peter 1 : 10–12, it is claimed that the ancient prophets prophesied by the Spirit, and the recipients of the letter have heard the Gospel from 'those who preached the good news to you through the Holy Spirit sent from heaven'. Then in the First Letter of John, the opening words claim that the writer is an authoritative witness to the revelation given from God in Christ.[65]

Paul claimed that what he preached was not the word of men but the Word of God, and that he gave instructions 'through the Lord Jesus'.[66] He claimed to be commissioned as an apostle of God, and to have received the gospel 'through a revelation of Jesus Christ'.[67] He imparted the message 'in words not taught by human wisdom but taught by the Spirit', and he wrote that 'if any one thinks that he is a prophet, or spiritual, he should acknowledge that what I am writing to you is a command of the Lord'.[68]

We have already seen the very great claims which the Epistle to the Hebrews makes for the Old Testament : the old covenant and the old revelation came from God, and the record of this is accounted as what God said. But his theme is that the new covenant and the new revelation are even greater than the old, seeing that the old came from God through prophets, but the new through His Son. If the Old Testament had supreme authority, the New should have, if it were possible, even greater.[69]

We have seen Temple's theory that in revelation we receive 'not truth concerning God but the living God Himself',[70] and Baillie's echo that God gives us not communication but communion.[71] But the New Testament *does* speak in terms of information being revealed, as well as God Himself. So there is 'the faith which was once for all delivered to the saints';[72] and Paul urged the Thessalonians to 'hold to the traditions which you were taught by us, either by word of mouth or by letter.[73] Similarly Timothy is urged to 'guard what has been entrusted to you',[74] or literally, 'guard the deposit', which, as the context shows, is the deposit of truth. The same idea occurs also in 2 Timothy : 'Guard the truth that has been entrusted to you by the Holy Spirit'; and Timothy is to pass this message on faithfully to other worthy teachers.[75] Further, Paul distinctly refers to revelation of facts : 'What no eye has seen, nor ear heard, nor the heart of man conceived, what God has prepared for those who love him, God has revealed to us through the Spirit.'[76]

VERBAL INSPIRATION?

The idea of the verbal inspiration of the Bible is not popular today; but popularity must not be confused with truth, and we may need to think again on such issues. It is often said that the Bible was accepted as the infallible, verbally inspired Word of God for many centuries, until biblical criticism began; and that since then such a view is impossible. But that is typical of the less favourable side of the radical approach: the total rejection of the old and the total acceptance of the new. It is becoming more apparent now, as a better perspective is possible, that biblical criticism in itself has not made the Bible into a purely human book. Writing on *The Authority of the Bible*, the Archbishop of Canterbury says: 'The methods and the conclusions of modern critical study may be shown to compel no denial of the authority of the Bible, but rather to assist our understanding of the ways in which it is *true, inspired* and the word of God in *revelation*.'[77] But these 'ways' are capable of different interpretation.

As we have seen, there has been a gradual return to the recognition that revelation consists in God speaking as well as acting. So Vincent Taylor concluded: 'The truth is we cannot avoid some theory of biblical inspiration if we are to find a worthy doctrine of revelation.'[78] Similarly James Barr finds: 'Direct verbal communication between God and particular men on particular occasions is, I believe, an inescapable fact of the Bible and of the Old Testament in particular. God can speak specific verbal messages, when He wills, to the men of His choice.'[79]

Those who reject the idea of the verbal inspiration of the Bible often call it a 'dictation theory'. Thus Zahrnt says: 'According to the orthodox understanding of Scripture, it was not developed and handed down like any other book; God Himself dictated it, and the writers, stripped of almost all human individuality, served only as automatic instruments of the Holy Spirit.'[80] Again he says: 'Thus the Bible did not suddenly lie one day on the altar at Jerusalem, complete'; it reflects the process of long historical growth.[81]

Now this sort of writing is really rather disgraceful. It is not at all a fair statement of the 'orthodox understanding', but it is a cheap parody. It is not a scholarly statement or argument, but a piece of authoritarian brow-beating. It is quoted here because students have to face this sort of parody, either in their lectures or in their reading. Zahrnt either is ignorant of, or misrepresents, 'orthodox understanding'. Those features which seem so objectionable in the 'orthodox understanding' are, in fact, not a part of the 'orthodox understanding' at all. So we find that B. B. Warfield, a scholarly defender of the 'orthodox understanding' of verbal inspiration, says : 'Of course, these books were not produced suddenly, by some miraculous act—handed down complete out of heaven, as the phrase goes; but, like all other products of time, are the ultimate effect of many processes cooperating through long periods. . . . And there is the preparation of the men to write these books to be considered, a preparation physical, intellectual, spiritual, which must have attended them throughout their whole lives. . . .'[82] Warfield adds : 'If God wished to give His people a series of letters like Paul's, He prepared a Paul to write them.'[83] And again : 'We are not defending a mechanical theory of inspiration. Every word of the Bible is the Word of God according to the doctrine we are discussing; but also and just as truly, every word is the word of a man. This at once sets aside as irrelevant a large number of the objections usually brought.'[84] Indeed, every one of the objections made in Zahrnt's parody was already answered by Warfield, long before Zahrnt wrote.

It is necessary to consider what is meant by God speaking, if the phrase is taken with its full meaning. Did those to whom God spoke hear an actual voice, in the same way that they would hear a human voice? First, we cannot deny that God could communicate thus if He so wanted. But it is not necessary to assume that there must have been a physical voice (that is, actual sound waves in the air) if the communication was verbal. When we hear an ordinary voice, the act of hearing is ultimately in the mind or brain.

In the same way, if a man of God 'heard' God, this would ultimately be in the mind or brain. Whether God spoke His Word directly to the mind or not, is a matter for conjecture, and is a matter of interest rather than of importance. The point here is that divine speaking does not necessarily have to be materialistic, and need not be ruled out on that account.

A further point is that a man normally thinks in words, and so any direct experience of God would in any case tend to be verbalized. There is no reason why we should not consider that God controlled this process, whether it was in 'hearing' God speak or writing God's Word. Thus, a man of God who has surrendered himself to God uses his own mind in thinking and writing, but he can at the same time be fully controlled by God.

PROOF

It is natural that we should enquire whether there is any proof that God has spoken and acted, and that the Bible is divinely inspired and authoritative. First we might ask what sort of proof would be desirable and convincing, and we may find that in the nature of the case no final proof is possible. But, if 'the fact of biblical inspiration cannot be verified by independent enquiry', as Packer reminds us, 'then neither can such facts as forgiveness or adoption'.[85] There is a simple logical problem: we can accept an authority on the basis of a higher authority, but if the Bible claims the highest authority for itself, namely, God's authority, then there is no higher authority to which we can appeal. Thus ultimately we can only either accept or reject this authority. Nevertheless, acceptance is not in the face of all reason.

The 'truth' of the Bible can be demonstrated only as far as it is an historical record. Thus archaeology can bring much evidence that events recorded in the Bible did actually happen. But it is not within the scope of archaeology to show that these events were acts of God. Nevertheless this evidence is important, as, negatively, if there were evidence that the events did *not* happen, then this would be a disproof. In other words, if the events did not happen, then clearly they were not acts of God.

The real proof is practical. If we accept it as fact that Jesus died and rose again, and if we accept it as divine revelation that Jesus died *for our sins* and that *God* raised Him from the dead, and if we accept it as a divine promise that through Jesus Christ crucified and risen we can receive forgiveness of sins, a new relationship with God and life of an eternal quality beginning now and never ending, then we find that we experience these things.

In one sense this is an act of faith which is a leap in the dark. But in fact it is not really 'in the dark'. For there is the witness of countless men and women throughout the centuries, from Abraham onwards, whose example we follow. Abraham simply took God at His word; and that was the faith by which he was justified, as we find in both the Old Testament[86] and the New.[87] Paul expounds this as the pattern of Christian faith, and the writer to the Hebrews traces examples throughout the Old Testament. It is because of these examples of faith that our faith is not entirely a blind leap in the dark.

Of course, faith in God is not the same as faith in the Bible. But it is faith in the God who has spoken in the Bible; and, throughout the centuries, God has spoken to men and women through the Bible. 'This', says Alan Richardson, 'is not an hypothesis or a dogma, but a statement of fact. The arguments to the contrary of those who have never heard God speaking are about as cogent as the attempts of a colour-blind man to prove that there is no difference between red and green.'[88]

In fairness to the author just quoted, it should be said that he repudiates any theory of verbal inspiration, which he explains as the dictation of the Holy Spirit and which he equates with fundamentalism.[89] But we have already shown that verbal inspiration is not necessarily dictation; rather it refers to God's control over the writing of the words being such that they say what He wishes them to say. And this is in effect what Alan Richardson says. What he is repudiating is in fact a dictation-theory, and not really verbal inspiration.

Further evidence of the inspiration of the Bible lies in the remarkable unity of its contents, to which we have already called attention.[90] While this is not a proof, nevertheless, in view of the wide diversity in the origin of the books of the Bible on any theory, the inspiration of the living God is the simplest explanation of that unity.

But the final proof for the Christian is in Christ Himself. It is Christ's attitude to the Scriptures (which for Him were the Old Testament) that must govern the Christian's attitude. It is difficult to see how a Christian can accept the authority of Christ without accepting the authority of Scripture which He acknowledged.

INSPIRATION AND THE CRITICAL APPROACH

We have already touched on this subject, but now, after our consideration separately of biblical criticism and of biblical inspiration and authority, we must return to it. We have seen the various assumptions and presuppositions which are often found in biblical criticism, and we have seen that the great presupposition of the Bible itself is the living God. We have noted that much biblical criticism must, by its very nature, be only speculation, reaching at the most a high degree of probability. We have argued also that the Bible makes great claims that God has both acted and spoken, and that the Bible claims to be given by the inspiration of the living God.

To accept that a certain book of the Bible was written under divine inspiration does not in itself show how or when the book was written. It does not preclude the use of sources, and it does not preclude the possibility of editing. Inspiration means that God was at work in the production of the book, but it does not necessarily indicate how. A dictation-theory would preclude all human elements, and therefore virtually preclude criticism. But the biblical view of inspiration is that God used human beings, as such, and that He used their minds.

It may seem to be difficult to accept that God could use fallible, sinful men and yet produce a verbally inspired Bible. W. H. Venable makes an interesting comparison with information-theory, showing that accurate information can be received from very distant space vehicles, as the unit is a complete sequence. Thus there is accuracy despite apparent failings.[91] This illustration may repay consideration.

There is a serious clash between biblical criticism and biblical inspiration only if either the criticism makes non-Christian, or unbiblical, assumptions, or uses methods which are not valid in themselves, or the view of inspiration is rigid in a way which is also unbiblical. In principal, there is no need for any clash. Of course, this may seem like a ludicrous oversimplification; but it must be remembered that there is not just one critical answer to all biblical problems, that scholars disagree amongst themselves, that theories change for various reasons, and that some of the theories, though bearing the names of worthy scholars, may be unacceptable because of their unacceptable presuppositions. What may be said with assurance is that no genuinely 'assured results' of biblical criticism have made acceptance of biblical inspiration and authority impossible. As was pointed out earlier,[92] when there is an apparent conflict, it is necessary to examine the basis of each of the apparently conflicting facts or theories. For this reason the student beginning Religious Studies is well advised to examine the basis for an acceptance of the Bible's inspiration and authority, reading at least some of the introductory literature on the subject,[93] this chapter being but the briefest outline. In view of the strength of this basis, it is more justifiable to suspend judgment than to capitulate to difficulties. Neither biblical criticism nor the doctrine of inspiration needs to be abandoned. With all his critical studies, the Christian can still use the Bible as the Word of God, and, as he reads it, meet the living God Himself.

Some Old Testament Problems

'Reading the Old Testament is like eating a large crab; it turns out to be mostly shell with very little meat in it.' Perhaps we feel some sympathy with this sentiment of a Chinese pastor.[1] And we are told by J. Bowden that 'in practice the Old Testament is losing its place by default'.[2] So often we hear that the Old Testament is primitive, and that the God of the Old Testament is not the God of the New; so that it is sometimes urged that we should abandon the Old Testament as obsolete.

This is no new suggestion: it was made by Marcion in the second century of the Christian era and he has had his followers throughout the centuries. But we can learn a lesson from Marcion: when he removed the Old Testament from his Bible, he found that he had to remove a considerable part of the New Testament also.[3] We cannot so easily sever the Old and the New, for we find that they have an 'organic connection'.[4] Indeed a current line of study which is increasing in popularity is known as 'salvation history', which views the saving acts of God as one continuous whole throughout the Old and the New Testaments.[5] And nearly twenty years ago, when Rowley wrote *The Unity of the Bible*,[6] he showed this close connection.

So important is the Old Testament for understanding the New, that Wright says: 'It is by the spectacles of the Old Testament that our eyes must be focussed upon the light in

Christ; otherwise that light will be blurred and we shall not see it correctly.'[7] Jesus Himself was a Jew brought up on the Old Testament, and Christianity was nurtured on the Old Testament from which it took over so much. It is the Old Testament which provides the language and sets the stage for the New.

But we must examine the connection more closely. It is often said that the relationship of the Old Testament to the New can be seen in the relationship or contrast between promise and fulfilment, law and grace, wrath and love. But in fact we find that the reverse order of these pairs is also true : we find fulfilment in the Old Testament and promise in the New; grace in the Old and law in the New; love in the Old and wrath in the New.[8] Though the emphases may be different, Old and New Testaments both contain each of these themes. So to set the Old in opposition to the New is very misleading. There is a progress in the self-revelation of the living God, but He is the same God who reveals Himself in Old and New Testaments. There are different stages of progress in the working out of the divine plan of salvation, from the beginning of the human race, the patriarchs, in the Exodus and Exile, the prophets and, finally, in God's Son. But He is the same saving God. The acts of mercy and of judgment occur throughout Old and New Testament.

If we think that judgment and wrath are characteristics of the Old Testament, we need to remember that these appear in the Gospels, in Jesus' words and actions (such as the cleansing of the Temple); in Acts (as in the deaths of Ananias and Sapphira); in the Epistles (as in Romans 1); and in the Revelation, where we get the remarkable picture of the wrath of the Lamb. Then in the Old Testament the message of the prophet Hosea about God's steadfast love and forgiveness has quite a New Testament ring about it.

We are sometimes told that the Old Testament God is portrayed in a primitive way. We may therefore heed the words of G. E. Wright: 'It is increasingly understood today that the former identifications in early Israel of a Mountain-God, a Fertility-God and a War-God, from which the "ethical

monotheism" of the prophets gradually evolved, are fig-
ments of scholarly presupposition and imagination.'⁹ Before
we are unduly disturbed by pronouncements about primitive
features in the Old Testament, it is wise always to see what
the Old Testament really does say. There are problems; but
many of them have, as Wright shows, arisen from a false
approach, which looked for, and then thought it found, these
primitive gods.

ANTHROPOMORPHISMS

The Old Testament frequently uses human terms in speaking about God. It speaks of His arm, His eyes, His mouth,
the breath of His nostrils, and of God speaking, visiting His
people, loving, and so on. These are terms which are
normally used with reference to human beings. Is this therefore a primitive view of God which we must reject? This
is no modern suggestion. Philo, the Alexandrian Jewish
scholar, tried 'to explain away the apparent anthropomorphism of God ... in favour of a philosopher's God'.¹⁰ But
a philosopher's God is only for philosophers, and is only an
object for philosophical argument. It may be observed that
Tillich, who removed all such anthropomorphisms for a
highly philosophical conception of God, was asked not long
before he died whether he prayed : he replied that he medit-
ated. Tillich could not have a personal relationship with
the sort of god he believed in.

By contrast, 'Israel's experience of God as a living Person
is understood by Israel's thinkers almost wholly in terms of
what it means to think, speak and act as a man. In Himself
God is unknowable. He is the "God who hides Himself
(Iasiah 45 : 15; Job 11 : 7; Psalm 97 : 2; Exodus 33 : 20).'¹¹
And Knight adds his comment on such anthropomorphism
'We dare not dismiss such pictorial thinking, simply on the
ground that it is "early " and "primitive". Pictorial thinking
is the essence of the whole biblical revelation. It is employed
in the NT just as much as it is in the OT.'¹²

We may notice also the words of G. E. Wright : 'Anthropomorphism thus indicates God's personal relation to his-

tory, and to assume that we can dispense with it as belonging to a primitive stage of our religious development is to separate ourselves not only from the Bible, but from the biblical conception of the true meaning of history.'[13]

A useful answer to the problem of anthropomorphism was made by Immanuel Kant nearly 200 years ago. He warned us not to try to go beyond the bounds of experience and think that, beyond these bounds, we can understand things as they are in themselves. Thus, he said, we do not attribute to God any of the properties 'by which we represent objects of experience, and we thereby avoid *dogmatic* anthropomorphism; but we attribute them to the relation of this Being to the world and allow ourselves a *symbolic* anthropomorphism'.[14] We find that we cannot avoid such symbolism, and to retain it is necessary if we are to think about God at all. Thus if we use human language about God, we do not imply that God is like a human being, but that we have a relation with Him in no less a way than with a human; the human language describes God-in-relation, not God-in-Himself.

SOME MORAL ISSUES

In various ways the moral standards found in the Old Testament present problems. First let us note the observations of John Bright: 'I find it most interesting and not a little odd that although the Old Testament on occasions offend our Christian feelings, it did not apparently offend Christ's "Christian feelings"! Could it really be that we are ethically and religiously more sensitive than He? Or is it perhaps that we do not view the Old Testament—and its God—as He did?'[15]

Before we investigate individual problems, it is desirable to get an over-all view of Old Testament morals. And we may find that they are other than we had thought. Every student of the Old Testament would do well to read the recent short book by Derek Kidner, *Hard Sayings: The challenge of Old Testament morals.*[16] In the first place, we find 'the challenge of what is outspoken and demanding, not merely what is problematic'.[17] It is salutary to bear in mind that the Old Testament was written as a guide to living, and not a book for studying. To feel the challenge is the best way to begin to understand it.

The Old Testament attitude towards God, Kidner reminds us, is one of fear, knowledge, trust and love. 'Love, it emerges, is commitment first, and sentiment only second. With this word, in fact, we reach the heart of Old Testament morality, since the basis of all its demands is personal: the living God.'[18] So Old Testament morality is basically 'loving obedience'. This is the highest possible basis for morality.

The real problems arise in connection with the stories of slaughter and war, and some of the violent imprecations, which do not seem to fit in with the New Testament picture of God. First, we have already noted that divine wrath and judgment appear in the New Testament also. So Knight well says: 'We have no right either to despise the ancient stories in the early books of the OT or to imagine that the ideas represented therein about the holy God may be dismissed as "primitive".... In contrast men today often speak lightly of the Creator of the heavens and the earth in chatty terms.... In thought and prayer they approach Him with careless irreverence.... So we turn from the significance of these stories at our peril.'[19] Thus instead of simply challenging these stories, we should first let them challenge us. The basic theology of them is God's great awe, majesty and holiness.

In much of our modern preaching we hear that God hates the sin, but loves the sinner. It may therefore come as a surprise to find, as Knight again points out,[20] that in the Old Testament 'the attitude of the all-holy God to sinful Israel is that of wrath against, not the sin, but the sinner... (Exodus 32:9-10; cf. Jeremiah 12:8)'. If we feel that we cannot really accept this, then it means that we do not have the same serious view of sin as the Old Testament—and indeed the New.

When we consider the so-called 'imprecatory psalms' (for

example, Psalm 83), the same issue arises. We may feel that we, if we are Christians, would not wish to use such imprecations; but we still need to remember 'the awful holiness of the righteous God'.[21]

It is often said that whereas the Old Testament said, 'An eye for an eye, and a tooth for a tooth',[22] Jesus contradicted this.[23] First we must notice that in its historical context the Old Testament law was an advance: retribution was limited to strict equivalence and no more. What Jesus said was that a better and a higher way is to exact no retribution at all. So here we see a progressively higher standard being applied.

A further example of a 'moral problem' of a different sort is seen in the case of Samson. He is depicted in the Old Testament as a judge, raised up by God and used by Him. But his life leaves very much to be desired, and he appears to be a man of unbridled passion. Yet he is listed in the New Testament[24] as one of those who did great exploits 'through faith'. But we can hardly be advised to follow his example. If we look at the rest of Scripture, clearly we cannot follow his example and are not meant to do so. However, we can see something of value. The Israelites were evidently in a low moral state, and Samson was at the same level. Nevertheless God used him. This does not imply that moral living does not matter, but that God can work through a human being even despite his imperfections. This is a lesson which can be very consoling. But included in the lesson is the fact that wrong *does* matter; for we see how Samson had to suffer as a direct consequence of his wrongs. Thus we see the balanced biblical picture of God's care for Israel, His mercy and His justice.

THE RITUAL LAWS

A practical question arises if we accept the Old Testament in the way that Christ did, as the inspired and authoritative Word of God: does it all apply to me? Should I, as a Christian, try to keep all the ritual or ceremonial laws of the Old Testament? The simple answer to this is that the

New Testament shows that the ceremonial law was fulfilled and completed in Christ, and so does not now apply to Christians. This may seem to nullify the whole idea of the inspiration and authority of Scripture. It may appear that information about the ceremonial law *was* authoritative, but is so no longer.

This is an inadequate way of looking at it, however. The ceremonial law needs first to be understood in its historical context. If God has progressively revealed Himself, we must find out what He has revealed about Himself in this sort of law. The utter holiness of God was shown to be such that a man could not just rush into His presence. The elaborate rituals were to make him approach with due care and reverence. This is surely a timeless truth about the nature of God. Even though the rituals do not apply now, the character of God is the same. This is an aspect of God's character which should be reflected in 'the fear of the Lord', which, as has already been said,[25] is at present largely ignored, and wrongly so. Thus it may be seen that the ceremonial law still has a message for us today.

INTERPRETING THE OLD TESTAMENT

There are some further points to remember about the interpretation of the Old Testament. Rowley warns us against a 'wooden literalism'.[26] Poetry must be read as poetry, for example, and perhaps the anthropomorphisms may be put into this category. But beyond this we have to read everything in its context. It has been said that a text without a context is a pretext. While it may be quite appropriate to quote odd verses which state clearly certain truths, there is always the danger that a verse quoted in isolation may be misleading. So, for example, in the book of Job there is a long discussion between Job and his 'comforters', and at the end of the book the 'comforters' are roundly rebuked for what they had said. Clearly therefore if we take an odd verse from one of the speeches of the 'comforters', this may be the opposite of the teaching of the book as a whole. If, therefore, we consider that this book is inspired by God, we must take the book as a whole, and interpret individual verses in the light of this. To accept the inspiration of the Bible does not mean to accept that every verse may be used as a proof text for something. Each verse must in the first place be understood in the light of its immediate context, and that must further be understood in the context of the whole book, and, again, that must be interpreted in the light of the whole Bible. It is this process which results in a 'theology of the Old Testament', and in a 'biblical theology'.

THE STORIES OF CREATION AND THE FALL

We have to face the issue of whether these stories are myth or history. If they are called 'myth', this implies that what is stated did not really happen; if, however, they are called 'history' and not 'myth', this may be taken to imply that they are literal accounts of what happened. It is better to avoid the term 'myth', as it is used in such varied senses.[27] At the very least, we can consider the stories as 'history' in the sense that creation 'really happened', and that God really did create the universe, the world and man.

The issue may be put in different terms: do these stories contain religious or scientific truth? The very form of the question prejudges certain matters, in assuming that religious and scientific truth are opposites, or that they are alternatives. The stories are not scientific in the sense that they are not intended as such. But if they are scientifically untrue, it is difficult to see that they can be religiously true. It is impossible to pretend that it is scientifically false and religiously true that God created everything. The statement is either true or false, but its *language* may be religious rather than scientific, and its *implications* may be in the realm of religion rather than science. Nevertheless, for our total understanding of the universe, religion and science must fit together, centring interest on different aspects, but not contradicting each other.

This may seem to imply that we accept from the biblical stories the *fact* of creation, but not the *method*; the outline, but not the details. Before reaching that conclusion, however, it is as well to examine the stories very carefully, and to see just what they do say—and what they do not say. It will be found that in Genesis 1 there is a most sublime and majestic account of God creating all; but we search in vain for any details of how He did it.

We shall consider briefly how to relate biblical and scientific ideas on the origin of the universe and the origin of man. First the universe : in outline, there are two competing scientific theories, the 'big bang' theory and 'continuous creation'. We are concerned here only with the general principles : according to the first theory, if we trace the history of the universe back in time, we arrive at zero time, the beginning, when there was an explosion of infinitely condensed matter. From this, the universe has been expanding and the present stars, sun and planets are explained. There is no real problem in principle in seeing in this how science and religion fit together. God created the first matter (as in Genesis 1) and He also created the explosion with all that followed. The scientific theory may be viewed as an attempt to describe how God created.

But with the other basic theory, that of continuous creation, it may at first seem more difficult. The theory suggests that there never was any beginning, and that creation of matter is still going on now, always has been and always will be. We need not attempt to elaborate any details of the theory. But certain points may be made. It is of interest to note that this theory *borrows* the term 'creation'. We can, in a way, understand some meaning in the statement 'God created'; but it is hard to see the meaning of the term 'creation' if there is no creator. We can only use the verb 'create' with a subject. But according to this theory, there is no creator. It would therefore be more accurate to call it the continuous 'appearance' of matter, and this leaves a large gap in the explanation. But the question is whether the theory of so-called continuous creation is compatible with the biblical story. E. L. Mascall, in his discussion of the subject,[28] points out that even if continuous creation is true, and there never was a beginning, we still need an explanation of why there is a universe at all. So even this theory is not contrary to the creation story, but requires it.

Our present concern is simply to show that there is no conflict in principle between science and religion in the doctrine of divine creation. So as regards the origin of the universe, we may say that from the Old Testament we find that God created it but we do not find how He did so; for that we turn to science.

The second question is the origin of man. This question is often posed as, 'Creation or evolution?' But to put the question that way is again to prejudge the issue, as it implies that these are two different and opposite ideas. Evolution is often described as if it were an explanation complete in itself, and as an alternative to believing in God. Now we must see that a scientific theory of evolution (whether true or false) cannot, as a scientific theory, preclude God. Again, we are concerned with the principles and not the details, and though, when the theory of evolution first appeared, it was strongly opposed by churchmen as being anti-Christian, to a large extent the battle has died down. There are some Christians who still ardently oppose evolution as a doctrine of the devil, and who consider that to accept evolution (in any sense) is an evil compromise and a rejection of the authority of the Bible. But many find that evolution and creation are not thus opposed. If evolution is true, then it is a description of how God created animals and man, and indeed every living thing.[29]

In the biblical story of the creation of man, we find two very important statements : God created man in His own image and God created man from the dust of the earth. So then man is linked with both the highest and the lowest. If we remember that we are basically dust, according to this account, then there is no real objection to an evolutionary theory that links us with animals. In one aspect, man is merely dust and merely an animal. It was by a creative act of God that man appeared; but whether in this act God took dust directly to create man, or used other creatures, is not clear from the Bible. The act of creation could, with the almighty God, take place equally easily in a split second or in millions of years. The 'six days' of the creation story do not assist our interpretation, as there is not the least certainty that they are meant as literal days; rather, many look upon these as simply a division of the creation into six parts. It may be noted that to interpret the 'days' as periods is not just a device for reconciling creation with evolution: Augustine made this interpretation about fifteen centuries ago.

The biblical doctrine of creation is not simply an account of the origin of things. It is a description of something vital about the nature of God, man and the universe, and the relation between God and man, God and the universe, and man and the universe. In the Bible, God is the living God, and this means that He is active, as a living Being, in the universe which He created, and that He *is* (not *was*) the Creator. The miracles and the supernatural in the Bible all fit in with this picture of God.[30] Also this is the living God with whom man, His creature, can enter into a personal relationship in response to His self-revelation.[31] Man is seen as linked with the material world in his body, and yet made in God's image, and to have dominion over God's world,[32] representing God in it. Man was not made an autonomous being (as is so often fondly imagined today), but a creature of God, whose true being and truest freedom were to be found in obedience to and fellowship with God. But things went wrong.

Closely linked with creation is the story of the fall. Man wanted to live independently of God his Creator, and to be autonomous; and the story of the fall is simply the story of disobedience to God. The result of this was that man was to know both good and evil by tasting of evil, and thus his nature became corrupted. As result of the fall we find man as a being made in God's image, but disobedient to Him; linked with both the dust and the living God, but having the link with God severed; made 'very good',[33] but become evil. So man today has a nature which is intrinsically good but tainted. This means that we find man capable of both the noblest and the basest deeds. It means too that man is sinful, and thus cannot meet God unless God in His grace offers a way of return; and also that man's mind is so affected that he cannot of himself know God.[34]

This story of the fall is basic to the whole Bible. After the perfect creation had gone wrong, there began the long process of God revealing Himself and His salvation, thus restoring man to fellowship with Himself.

Again, we have to face the problem about taking the story of the fall literally. In a way, this is not as big a problem as it might appear. For whether we take the story as literally true or as symbolically true, the final result is the same : man is a fallen creature, with an unrealized potential, and standing in need of God's revelation and God's salvation. If we accept the authority of the Bible, we are bound to accept it as fact that God created man and that man fell : but we may be unsure of precise details, which are, after all, not important.

It appears, then, that the first chapters of the Bible, which may at first sight seem to be so hard to accept, are not only intelligible, but of fundamental importance. If carefully considered, the problems disappear. The clash with science is not due to a fundamental discrepancy between the Bible and science, but to beginning with preconceived ideas. What we find in Genesis is neither science nor myth, but the very Word of God.

Christ & Criticism

Perhaps one of the most disturbing parts of Religious Studies for the student is Christology—the examination of the question of who Jesus Christ really was and is. It is disturbing because, for the Christian, the very centre and foundation of his faith and life may seem to be challenged. This is no reason for avoiding the study—but rather for facing it. For if Christianity is true it will stand up to any test; if it is false, then the sooner we find out the better. The Christian whose beliefs have been put through a rigorous examination, and who has survived the ordeal, is in a very strong position. It may be worth remembering that Christianity and the person of Christ have been the object of attacks from the beginning, and have survived, triumphant.

THE HUMAN JESUS

But it is not only the subject itself which may be disturbing: it is the presentation of it. It is often said these days that in the past the divinity of Jesus has been stressed so much that His humanity has been almost ignored: He has been portrayed like God dressed up as a man; so, we are told, we need to redress the balance; and in practice this means going to the opposite extreme. Thus Zahrnt tells us that certainly Jesus Christ is 'more than a man'; he accepts the old formula 'true man' and 'true God'; but he adds that ' " true man" must now be understood to keep Jesus strictly within the bounds of what is historical and therefore historically possible, and likewise the expression "true God" must be interpreted in such a way that it does not do away with any historically admissible understanding of the "true man"'; and so he insists that 'Jesus as Son of God involves nothing "suprahistorical", "supernatural", or even unnatural'.[1] Thus, after admitting Jesus' divinity, the robs the words of all meaning and makes Jesus purely human.

For another example we may look at P. N. Hamilton's 'Some Proposals for a Modern Christology'.[2] After admitting insoluble problems in 'explanations' of the resurrection,[3] he proceeds to state his logic: an action is either God's or man's, and it cannot be both; whatever else we know, Jesus was a man; therefore His actions were human, and therefore they were not divine, but only in 'sympathy' with God.[4] He adds: 'Nothing must impair our accompanying belief in the manhood of Jesus'[5] and says that it is logic 'which insists that one cannot both describe Jesus as a man and also say that God's indwelling in him differs in kind from his indwelling in other men'.[6]

A LOGICAL ARGUMENT?

At this point let us note simply the basis for the purely human figure of Jesus: it is 'logic', in the case of both writers quoted. And this 'logic' is a pure assumption, and begs the whole question of whether Jesus was unique and, if so, in what way. The assumption is that because Jesus was human, He could not be anything more than human; in other words, it is a question of either *only* human or *not* human. To assume that we may settle this matter entirely by 'logic' is to assume the complete autonomy of the human mind, and to deny entirely the need for revelation. Thus it is entirely opposed to the biblical view of God and man; 'for my thoughts are not your thoughts, neither are your ways my ways, says the Lord. For as the heavens are higher than the earth, so are my ways higher than your ways and my thoughts than your thoughts'.[7] C. S. Lewis shrewdly commented on such logic: 'We, being men, know what we think : and we find the doctrines of the Resurrection, the Ascension, and the Second Coming inadequate to our thoughts. But supposing these things were the expressions of God's thought?'[8] We may find that to call Jesus truly human and truly divine goes against our human logic : but we need to know whether this could be God's logic. All the issues which we have mentioned in Religious Studies are relevant to the problems of Christology : presuppositions, miracles and the supernatural, the resurrection of Christ, biblical criticism, history and the question of divine revelation.

The first point which the student needs to remember in studying Christology is that there is no unanimity of scholarship, even though he may find himself presented with one set of conclusions as being *the* scholarly view of the evidence. The idea of 'the assured results of modern scholarship' is now very antiquated, as one set of 'assured results' gives way to another. In despair the student may wonder with Pope, 'Who shall decide, when Doctors disagree?' It is important to read books from differing points of view, and especially some books which offer a critique of what may be presented as the accepted view. To read only one book on the subject, such as Fuller's,[9] is to get a very distorted view of the subject; and it is advisable to read also something more conservative, such as Cullmann[10] and Carl Henry,[11] and to consider the views of such as Moule[12] and Marshall.[13] It is equally narrow-minded to read only liberal/radical books as it is to read only conservative books; and the New Testament Theology of Conzelmann[14] needs to be balanced with that of Jeremias,[15] scholars equally radical in their methods and thinking, but differing in their conclusions.

SOME MAJOR ASSUMPTIONS

Our concern here is to do no more than consider the methods, approaches and assumptions of Christology today, as an introductory guide to further study. As Fuller claims to give *The Foundations of New Testament Christology*, we shall examine his view of those foundations.

Fuller begins by stating his own 'theological presuppositions': the first is that Christology is 'a confession of faith', 'a response to a particular history' and 'is not in itself a part of the original revelation or action of God in Christ'.[16] This is really rather remarkable, as he decides in advance, by a presupposition, the answer to the whole problem; Christology is not something disclosed by God but discovered by man, and it comes not from Christ but from the church. It seems to be the assumption, before examining the evidence, that we shall not find in the Gospels a Christology coming directly from Christ. The second major presupposition follows from this: the Gospels tell us directly not about Jesus when He was on earth, but about the theology of the church after Jesus had left the earth. This, of course, is a common assumption now, but it is still an assumption. It will follow that we cannot take anything in the Gospels at its face value, as it is liable to have been either modified, or even invented, by the church.

However popular these two great assumptions may be, and whatever the brilliance of argument used to elaborate them, they remain assumptions, and indeed remarkable assumptions when we consider that the net result is that we have to make the evidence say the opposite to what it appears to say. It is not surprising therefore to find Professor Langmead Casserley writing of 'the ineptitude of modern theology'.[17]

The third great assumption is that there were distinct and separate stages of development in the beliefs of the early church. Bultmann sharply distinguished the early church and the Hellenistic church, considering the latter to be responsible for importing Greek ideas into Christianity. Hahn elaborated and made three stages before Paul, and Fuller has followed this. There are supposed to be first Palestinian Christianity, then Hellenistic Jewish Christianity, and finally Hellenistic Gentile Christianity. It is claimed that Christianity developed in these three distinct stages and moreover that 'critical presuppositions and methods ... enable us to distinguish between the various strata of tradition'.[18] The result of this assumption is that some writers 'have strongly emphasized that in the earliest forms of Christology there was no idea that Jesus had a divine nature and that in a Palestinian milieu this idea would have been unthinkable'.[19] So Fuller says: 'The very idea of incarnation, with its corollary of pre-existence, was quite foreign to the Christology of the earliest church';[20] and he thinks that earlier statements only show what Jesus *did*, not what He *was*; it was not until the gentile mission that Christianity spoke of what Jesus *was*.[21]

The implication of this is very great indeed; for it follows that Jesus is not really what the New Testament says He is. The lofty picture of the incarnate Son of God as presented throughout the New Testament, directly or indirectly, is written off as a later accretion, and we are left with a man who was deified by followers more creative than himself.

ARE THE ASSUMPTIONS WELL FOUNDED?

We must ask what is the basis for the assertion that there were separate Gentile churches which developed independently of the Jewish Christian communities. Neill sums up the situation: Conzelmann twice admits that there is no evidence in any of our sources that any such separate Gentile churches existed; 'everything that we say about them depends on more or less precarious inference'; and he adds that it is a 'strange result' that Bultmann writes 100 pages on 'the life and thought of these Gentile communities of which we cannot certainly know that they ever existed'.[22]

The evidence is in fact just the reverse of what would be required for the separate communities imagined by Bultmann and Fuller. 'We have no evidence', says Neill again, 'of any Christian community in the world which was not founded on the Old Testament.... The idea that there were groups here and there who were unaffected by this relatedness of the Church to the Old Testament, and who worked out their doctrine of the Christ independently in Hellenistic terms and in categories that had nothing to do with the Old Testament, rests on no evidence whatever.'[23]

The theory is one of the evolution of Christology; and, as Moule points out,[24] this depends on the assumptions not only of separate communities, but of chronological sequence; and though different communities may have had different emphases, 'it does not necessarily follow that there was a straight evolution from "low" to "high", or that a high Christology is not a true description of Jesus as He was from the beginning, or that one particular type came from one particular quarter'.

We have already referred to the unity in the Bible; and in particular the unity of the New Testament is important here. For we find a remarkable similarity of thought even though it may be expressed in different terms. So Hunter, writing on this unity nearly thirty years ago, found 'one common religious attitude to Jesus ... for one and all "Jesus is Lord" '.[25] He added moreover : 'Paul's essential Christology is not fundamentally different from that of the Primitive Church', as may be seen by comparing Acts 2 : 21 with Romans 10 : 13, and Acts 4 : 12 with Corinthians 3 : 11.[26]

A further point of great importance is the question of time. Paul is supposed to show the highest stage of the development, and yet this earlier writings, which show his full Christology, came only twenty years after the church began. An ancient historian, Sherwin-White, confesses that he is most surprised at 'the presumed tempo of development'.[27] The time seems to be quite inadequate for such a theory to be feasible.

WHAT IS AUTHENTIC?

Next we must consider the proposed methods of deciding what material in the Gospels is authentic (from Jesus Himself) and what is not. This is a subject still being discussed and elaborated. Fuller asserts that if a saying attributed to Jesus had as parallel in Jewish tradition or if it reflects the 'faith, practice and situations' of the church as it was after the first Easter, then that saying is not authentic.[28] Now this is highly arbitrary. To assert that Jesus did not pronounce a saying just because it has a Jewish parallel is totally unrealistic. There is no reason why Jesus should not have said such things. Again, to show that a saying *could* fit into the life of the early church is no proof whatever that it *must* fit there, and that it cannot fit into the life of Jesus. The whole argument that any saying 'reflects' such and such a community is highly tendentious.[29]

We may look at an example of the principle being applied. In discussing the heavenly voice at Jesus' baptism, which refers to Jesus in terms of the 'servant', Fuller says that the early church thought of Jesus in terms of the servant, and 'therefore the heavenly voice must be set to the credit of the earliest Palestinian church, rather than to Jesus' personal reminiscence of his baptismal experience'.[30] He adds : 'It cannot be used as evidence for Jesus' self-understanding.'

This type of argument is quite unconvincing : in fact, it is not an argument at all : it is just an assertion. No reason is given why the church should not have obtained the idea from Jesus; it is pure speculation that the church invented the idea and then put it into the baptismal story. We wish to know what was the source of the church's inspiration, if not Jesus Himself.

THE TITLE 'SON OF MAN'

A further example to consider is Fuller's treatment of the title 'Son of Man'. This is now the centre of much debate, and we may look at some features of it. Fuller tells us : 'Jesus could not identify himself with the coming Son of Man, since that figure was to come at the End on the clouds of heaven.'[31] Rather, Fuller thinks that Jesus understood that His own mission would be vindicated by the Son of Man at the end.[32] In his review of the book, I. H. Marshall comments that if Jesus did not identify Himself with the Son of Man, but the church did, this implies that Jesus was mistaken and the church falsified the facts, by imposing divine self-conscious into Jesus.[33] Again, Fuller's inverting of the evidence to make it say the opposite of what it appears to say is unwarranted, unproved and unlikely. It is a very high-handed way to treat literature.

Fuller considers, following Bultmann, that 'there is an inner inconsistency within the Son of Man sayings'.[34] He makes no attempt to reconcile the apparent inconsistencies, but simply assumes that many of the sayings cannot be genuine. By contrast, Morna Hooker examines all the Son of Man sayings in Mark, and finds that they do cohere and make a consistent picture.[35] An explanation which makes sense of all the sayings is more likely to be true than one which makes nonsense of them : it is better to explain the evidence than to dispose of it.

Those who do not accept these sayings as genuine assume that they were produced by the church, and there are remarkable displays of ingenuity in explaining their origin, by such as Colpe[36] and Perrin.[37] Conzelmann is an example of an extreme radical critic in this. He quickly dismisses arguments for the genuineness of the sayings, and then proceeds to dispose of them either in groups or individually. Thus he categorically asserts that the sayings which predict Jesus' sufferings were prophecies written after the event; sayings about the Son of Man on earth are dismissed one by one, mostly in a sentence, on the grounds that they are dogmatic and therefore were produced by the church; and of the sayings about the future Son of Man, two come from Daniel and so are assumed to be unauthentic (though the reason for this is not obvious), one is for comfort in persecution, and so is assumed to have originated in the church, and that leaves only Mark 8 : 38. After stating that 'there is a wide-ranging consensus that this saying is authentic', Conzelmann finds it to be incomprehensible on the lips of Jesus and so he dismisses this also.[38] To those who are already convinced that Christian theology came from the church and not from Christ, the disposal of all the evidence in this way may be pleasing; but to those who are not convinced that the church was more creative than its Creator, his arguments seem extremely thin and unconvincing. We can see no reason why Jesus could not predict His death;

because a saying has relevance to the church, that is no proof that it must have originated in the church; because a saying quotes Daniel, that is no reason for Jesus not uttering it; if a saying was of comfort in persecution, that is a good reason for preserving a genuine saying and no proof that it was composed for the later persecution; and what is 'incomprehensible' for Conzelmann is quite comprehensible for others. It appears that Conzelmann has decided in advance that all the sayings originated in the church, and then he tried to find evidence for this.

HOW MUCH IS AUTHENTIC?

This leads to the basic question of whether, from a critical point of view, the material in the Gospels may be considered reliable. The differences of opinion here are immense. Thus Perrin starts with the dictum that the burden of proof must lay (*sic*) on the claim to authenticity.[39] In other words, we are to assume that a saying ascribed to Jesus is unauthentic until it is proved authentic. This highly sceptical attitude is not shared by all. So Jeremias says just the opposite; as a result of his examination of the linguistic and stylistic evidence, he concluded: 'In the synoptic tradition it is the inauthenticity, and not the authenticity, of the sayings of Jesus that must be demonstrated.'[40] In other words, we are to assume that a saying ascribed to Jesus is authentic until it is proved otherwise. It should be noted particularly that Jeremias does not write his dictum from a conservative predilection, but from his reading of the evidence; and moreover it is only fair to add that he does not assume that all the sayings are genuine, but rejects some.

It is, of course, a recognized part of the critical approach to the Gospels to consider the authenticity of the material. The attempt is not made to prove that at all, in its entirety, is either true or false, but to consider each item separately. But we see that there are basically opposite starting-points. It is observed that nothing is said of the work of the Holy Spirit in the preservation of the sayings. Anyone who accepts this will not lightly dismiss the tradition in the Gospels as basically unauthentic. Nevertheless, acceptance of the work of the Holy Spirit does not remove the need to examine the sayings very carefully. If they are indeed authentic, they will stand up to the test. What is conspicuous in the writings of those who find so much of the material unauthentic is the specious nature of some of the arguments, and the frequency of highly tentative assumptions. The reader needs only to look at almost any page of Fuller to see this. Words such as 'clearly' and 'obviously' do not constitute any proof at all. Thus we find that when Fuller considers the term 'Son' or 'Son of God' referring to Jesus' understanding of Himself, he dismisses one use with the word 'perhaps', another with 'probably' and another with 'inclined to think'.[41] It seems that he has decided in advance that the titles ascribed to Jesus were not authentic.

So we find that modern criticism has made some very severe attacks on the authenticity of sayings ascribed to Jesus, and whereas once our view of the person of Jesus could be decided simply by examining these titles, the critical approach has rejected many of them. Nevertheless it must be pointed out that this is far from the unanimous opinion, and the weight of scholarship is not all on the side of rejection.

EXAMINING THE EVIDENCE

If we find doubt cast upon whether Jesus used the title Son of Man, and the suggestion that its use is due to the church, then we find one great stumbling-block in the way of this theory: from all the evidence we have, the church did not use this title. In Acts it occurs only once, and that is a special case.[42] All the evidence is that Jesus used the title Himself, no-one in the Gospels used it in addressing Him or talking of Him, and the church did not use it. There is no reason to explain why the church should ascribe the title to Jesus if neither He nor the church used it. Moreover, its use by Jesus during His lifetime and the discontinuance of its use then is shown to make sense.[43]

The test of the theory that the Gospels show the faith

of the church rather than the authentic sayings of Jesus can be made by comparing the two writings of Luke, the Gospel and the Acts. Moule[44] and Marshall[45] have done this with important results. It appears that Luke carefully distinguished between the periods before and after the resurrection. So in the Gospel, as Luke sees Lordship conferred on Jesus at the resurrection, he as narrator uses the term 'Lord' of Jesus, but he does not put it on the lips of men. But the word is used immediately after the resurrection,[46] and then regularly in Acts. This is strong evidence for the reliability of the Gospel material as regards the use of the titles.

APART FROM THE TITLES

However, our estimate of the person of Jesus does not depend only on the titles which are ascribed to Him in the Gospels. Quite apart from the titles, the whole picture of Jesus is such that E. Schweizer calls one of his chapters : 'Jesus : the Man Who Fits No Formula'.[47] And Moule comments : 'It looks as though here was one who perhaps seldom or never expressly *claimed* a title for himself except that of the suffering and eclipsed martyr Son of Man; but who *behaved* with the mastery appropriate to one who was heir to the whole kingdom, and who occasionally lifted the veil of his self-consciousness to reveal just this at the heart of his vocation.'[48]

The evidence that Jesus used the Aramaic word *Abba* (Father) when addressing God has been shown by Jeremias to be very great and very important.[49] Jesus used the term in all His prayers, in all the Gospel strands of tradition. It seems that the word was never used thus by the Jews, but was unique on the lips of Jesus. Quite apart from any use of the word 'Son', His use of *Abba* is the clearest possible demonstration of Jesus' awareness of a unique relationship with God as His Father. The fact that the early Christians used the word *Abba*[50] in Aramaic, though they spoke Greek, is confirmation that the word goes back to Jesus Himself. The Christian use depends on Jesus : as He is *the* Son, who can truly address God as Father, Christians in Him can enter into the same relationship. It is notable that though Jesus said, 'My Father' and 'Your Father', He never said, 'Our Father'; and thus He indicated that His Sonship was unique, never equating others with Himself in this.

Another small but important Aramaic word is *Amen*. This was used frequently by Jews at the end of their prayers, as we use it; but Jesus uniquely used it at the beginning of some of His great pronouncements. This shows 'Jesus' extraordinary sense of personal authority';[51] and it has been remarked that this little word contains in a nutshell the whole of Christology.[52] The fact that Christians did not accept this usage themselves is strong evidence of the genuineness of the word on the lips of Jesus Himself.

Another saying of Jesus may be considered : His call, 'Come to me'.[53] In the Old Testament the prophets constantly called the people back to God; they would only use such words as directly from God Himself. The prophets did not call people to themselves, but to God. But Jesus here speaks as God Himself. This is a further example of the sublime authority implicit or explicit in Jesus' words and deeds.

THE RESURRECTION

The resurrection of Jesus is the vital and ultimate fact which has to be considered in Christology. Fuller has written a book in which he tries to dispose of the miracles except in as far as they have purely natural explanations,[54] and it is therefore not surprising to find, in his study of Christology, that he has a minimal view of the resurrection. He says that the resurrection 'means that God took Jesus out of the past into his own eternal contemporaneity'.[55] All we need say (after our previous discussion of this subject) is that this interpretation has little to do with the New Testament. It is another way of saying that Jesus did not rise again. By contrast Moule sees the resurrection as real and basic, as he shows in his *Phenomenon of the New Testament* : without the resurrection there would have been no church and no New Testament. It is no accident that Fuller and Moule have opposite views of the resurrection and opposite views of Christology. Despite such as Fuller, Moule says : 'Thus, qualify the statement as one may (and, indeed, must), it is true that some not inconsiderable groups of scholars are daring once more, in a sense, to look back to the Jesus of history; but now they are finding, not the Liberal Protestant figure but a figure as challenging, as supernatural, as divine, as is found on the hither side in the apostolic gospel.'[56]

So the student may take heart! If modern scholarship has made an assault on the person of Christ, and if some scholars try to debunk the message which the New Testament appears to give about Him, others, little by little, by equal scholarship, are finding that His person stands as firm and sure as ever. An honest scholar cannot just accept the conclusions that please him and reject those that do not. What he can and must do is to examine not just the conclusions, but the way they are reached. It is hoped that the student who reads this chapter will read it in the light of every other chapter. He will find that, far from shattering his faith, a careful and thorough study of Christology, pursued with a faith in the living God who has acted and spoken in the past, will lead him into a deeper faith, to exclaim with Thomas, on seeing Jesus risen from the dead, 'My Lord and my God!'

Some Practical Issues

In Christian studies the Bible has a distinctive place. Though there are widely differing views on the degree of authority which it has, nevertheless it is generally held to have at least some authority. But if we recognize the Bible as having some authority in a distinctive way, we have to face the question of why we have this particular set of books in the Bible, neither more nor less. This is the question of the Canon of Scripture.

In his book, *What about the Old Testament?*, John Bowden expresses his opinion that the Bible has its special status 'as a result of the church's decision, like that of Judaism earlier in the case of the Old Testament, that here was a definitive record and criterion'.[1] This is an inaccurate statement, and is of a sort not uncommon. It is said that the church gave authority to the Bible. Bowden goes on to question whether the decision about the Canon is irreversible, and considers that it is not; so he quotes with approval that we need not only 'reform by the word of God', but also 'reform of the word of God'.[2] Now this is really quite extraordinary. Certain books either are, or they are not, the Word of God; and the suggestion that we could 'reform the word of God' is meaningless. Bowden shows his own misunderstanding of what the Canon really is, as well as his inaccurate statement about its formation.

A rather more accurate statement is made by the Archbishop of Canterbury in his article on 'The Authority of the Bible' in Peake's Commentary: 'Though the Church made the Canon of the New Testament, it was not thereby conferring authority on the Books. Rather it was acknowledging the Books to possess authority in virtue of what they were, and it was an authority supreme and divine.'[3] Similarly, John Bright: 'Certain books which had come to be regarded as having peculiar authority were selected as canonical Scripture';[4] and 'In establishing the canon the church did not create a new authority, but rather acknowledged and ratified an existing one. Books were selected because they were already recognized as authoritative.'[5]

It is sometimes said that the limits of the Canon of the Old Testament were settled by the Jewish Synod of Jamnia in AD 90. In fact, however, that synod did not decide on the Old Testament Canon as a new thing, but simply decided that the books already recognized were rightly recognized. The exact process of the growth of the Old Testament Canon is not known; and we shall not attempt to trace here what is known. But it appears that little by little the books came to be recognized as having authority.

Similarly with the New Testament, there was a formal acknowledgment of the full New Testament Canon in Athanasius' paschal letter of AD 367. But this did not make the Canon: it recognized a Canon already existing. The books which we have in our New Testament came to be recognized, from their own nature and intrinsic worth, as authoritative. So Moule, writing about the acceptance of our four Gospels, says: 'Its formal declaration, when it was made, was only the recognition, by the Church collectively, of a conviction that had long been silently growing on their consciousness.'[6]

Now if we consider what it means that the Bible is the Word of God,[7] then the different books in the Bible are the Word of God because God overruled the writing of them. The inspiration of Scripture, as we have seen,[8] means that God 'breathed them out', and not that some authority was given to some purely human books. So the formation of the Canon was the recognition of this inspiration in certain books.

If we wish to check for ourselves whether the right decision was made in selecting the New Testament books, we can look at the books which were *not* accepted or recognized. These are published as *The Apocryphal New Testament*.[9] The nature of them is seen to be quite different. Thus for example there are stories of miracles quite unlike New Testament miracles; these are simply like magic, with no purpose. So Moule writes: 'There is no known extra-canonical Gospel material which is not (when it can be tested at all) in some way subject to suspicion for its genuineness or its orthodoxy.'[10]

The question arises as to whether there had to be any limit to the Canon: could not valuable books be added indefinitely? After all, there have been great spiritual classics written throughout the centuries. It is not to be denied that there are such spiritual classics, and that they are of great value. But we must consider the nature of their value and authority. They do not tell us more than the Bible does, and the authority they have is itself derived from the Bible; their great value is ultimately in the exposition and application of what is already in the Bible. Such books may well be considered as inspired; but the inspiration claimed for the biblical books is not only greater, but of a different category.

In the Bible we have something complete. The Old Testament (or Covenant) looks forward to something new to come, and the seal of its authority was set by Christ Himself. The New Testament proclaims not only *a* new part of God's plan, but the last stage of it. The New Testament proclamation is that the last days, as foretold in the Old Testament, have already dawned. With the coming of Christ, the New Age began, and the New Testament is the primary witness to this.[11] There is now nothing really new to come until the final consummation of this age, at the end of time. Christ is God's 'last word'.

So then in the Bible we find the Word of God, complete. This is no arbitrary limit, but follows from the nature of God's salvation and self-revelation. It is no cramping limitation; for, as the centuries have shown, there is more than enough therein to occupy a man for a lifetime. There is the constant need to understand, and to reinterpret for the present generation. But it is a reinterpretation of what has already and adequately been given. The constant demand in some circles for 'something new' is not a sign of spiritual maturity or of a 'world come of age', but of a lingering adolescence. It is enough that 'in many and various ways God spoke of old to our fathers by the prophets; but in these last days he was spoken to us by a Son'.[12]

THE PURPOSE OF THE BIBLE

'Many critical scholars', Ladd reminds us, 'have been so enamoured of the discovery that the Bible is in fact the words of men written within the historical process that they have often neglected altogether the significance of the Bible as the Word of God.'[13] If we are prepared to accept the Bible's claims for itself, and that on the authority of Christ Himself, then we have a book which is both human and divine. If we reject any mechanical idea of divine dictation, then we recognize the human side of the Bible, and must give this full consideration. We welcome biblical criticism as a means to explore the Bible; but we do not necessarily welcome every method that has been employed. Our recognition of the divine side of the Bible prevents our acceptance of those critical methods or arguments which directly deny the activity of the living God, as in prediction or in supernatural events. But as we study the human aspects of the Bible, we must not disregard the divine side, and so we need to consider just why the Bible was written, what its purpose is, and what it means to consider it as the Word of God.

It is often said that the Bible is not a scientific textbook, and that we do not turn to it to learn science. But it may even be said also that, ultimately, the Bible is not a theological textbook, and we should not turn to it just to learn theology. The claim made in the Bible is that God has made a revelation in order that man may obey God and live in a right way before Him. 'The secret things belong to the Lord our God; but the things that are revealed belong to us and to our children for ever, that we may do all the words of this law.'[14] Similarly in the New Testament: 'All scripture is inspired by God and profitable for teaching, for reproof, for correction, and for training in righteousness, that the man of God may be complete, equipped for every good work.'[15]

So Knight says: 'It is not sufficient to say that the Old Testament is a book *about* God. It would be more correct to say that the Old Testament is the book through which God speaks and reveals His will.'[16]

We have to recognize the human and the divine sides of the Bible together when we try to understand it as the Word of God. For we do not simply find in it a set of statements about God's character and will. We have already mentioned the question of interpretation.[17] A further aspect is that God has revealed His will to certain individuals in certain particular situations. We have to examine the situation and find out the principles involved in the revealed will of God, and apply the principles; the exact details may not be the same in our society as in ancient society. Thus, for example, the instruction given that women should wear veils[18] has to be read in the light of the significance of wearing, or not wearing, veils in Corinth in the first century; and it does not follow that women ought to wear veils today. They are no longer a sign of respectability. Acceptance of the Bible as the Word of God does not mean a literalistic understanding; it involves careful study to obtain the proper meaning. This is not a way of evading the commands of the Bible, but of seeing what they really mean for us today.

The doctrine of inspiration states that the Holy Spirit of God was at work in the writers who penned Scripture; but it is of equal importance to remember that the work of the Holy Spirit is also needed in the interpretation of Scripture. It is not a 'dead letter'. So we find that as God has spoken in Scripture, so He speaks in our hearts: 'It is the God who said, "Let light shine out of darkness," who has shone in our hearts to give the light of the knowledge of the glory of God in the face of Christ.'[19] And our Lord Himself promised that the Holy Spirit would reveal Him.[20] As there is the human and the divine side to Scripture, so there is the human and the divine side to understanding Scripture: we to make our historical critical study, and we also need the aid of the Holy Spirit.

THE USE OF THE BIBLE

From the consideration of the purpose of the Bible there follows the implication that a study of the Bible just to learn, and not to live, is wrong, and is a misuse of the Bible. This may seem a strange statement, but it must follow if we take the Bible at all seriously.

The earliest Christian confession, as Cullmann reminds us in his book with that name, was simply 'Christ is Lord', and this was a confession parallel with the official creed, 'Caesar is Lord'.[21] So being a Christian basically meant obedience to Christ as Lord in one's life. The rule of Christ was to be as real as the rule of Caesar. So study of the Bible should ultimately be to find out and to obey the will of God and of His Son.

In writing about his work of translating the New Testament, J. B. Phillips repeatedly remarked that the Scriptures seemed to be alive. But he warned that 'it is horribly possible so to dissect your subject that you remove its life. By the time each source and component has been tagged and labelled this vibrant and compelling body is no more than a cadaver on the theological operating-table.'[22]

In practical terms, therefore, every time the student learns something from the Bible, or writes an essay, he should ask himself, How should this affect my life? To write an essay on the holiness of God as in Isaiah should be a shattering experience, just as the vision was for Isaiah himself.[23]

The point being made is that Religious Studies cannot properly be put on the same level as any other subject. The study requires the same mental discipline and thorough scholarship as any other subject, or perhaps even more, because of the wide compass of the subject. But it cannot be treated purely objectively without personal risk. God is 'Thou', not 'It'. He is to be encountered, not just discussed.

There are two types of knowledge : one is the knowledge of things and the other is the knowledge of persons. We can know *about* a person in the same way as we can know about a thing. But to know a person is a far deeper thing. It signifies having a relationship. To know theology is the former sort of knowledge; to know God is the latter. Of course, the two are not entirely distinct, but to know theology without knowing God is a terrible fate. It is a sorrowful fact that such a thing is not rare. But to know God and His Son is eternal life.[24]

An interesting 'parable' was told by Eddington[25] of the man who fished in the sea with a net of two-inch mesh; when he examined his catch, he propounded the theory that no fish existed that were less than two inches long! Science 'fishes' with a certain type of net, and gathers a certain type of information only. But the same may be applied to the different methods used in studying the Bible. The literary critic finds only sources such as he seeks; the form critic finds oral forms in the tradition; the redaction critic finds only the theology of the writers he examines (and not the history of the events described); the historian however finds history; the existentialist interpreter finds only an existential interpretation of life; the one who approaches the Bible with an open and obedient heart finds there the Word of the living God. When we consider all these approaches together, we do not need to decide which we shall have : rather we can use each approach, and add together the benefits derived from each. The great problems arise if we choose one approach only and assume that what we gain from that one approach is the whole truth. It may be justifiable to say that the different approaches are right in what they affirm but wrong in what they deny. Thus to affirm that the writers of the Gospels were theologians is right; but to deny therefore that what they recorded was history does not follow. Similarly to recognize the human aspects of the way the Bible was written does not make it any less the Word of God. Moreover, study of the Bible as part of an official study should not make it any less the means through which the living God speaks to us.

A point of practical importance is that it is very easy, in biblical studies, to read books about the Bible and not to read the Bible itself. The older biblical criticism was obsessed with origins and largely ignored the contents of the biblical books. The growth of biblical theology is a reaction against this. Its purpose is to find out what the Bible really says. But even here it is possible to read books about biblical theology without reading the Bible itself. The study then becomes not what the Bible says, but what various scholars say the Bible says. This is a trap as much for the lecturer as for the student. It is always worth going back to the original sources—in this case, the Bible. After all, the real source of Christology is neither Cullmann nor Fuller nor any other, but the New Testament.

A student may find that his own point of view is very different from that of his lecturer. This may present difficult problems. In the first place the student should recognize and respect the greater knowledge of the one who should be teaching him. But this does not mean that he must necessarily accept all that he says. If he disagrees, he should consider carefully why this is so. Different views on the authority of the Bible, or on miracles, lead to quite different views on many other matters. The student will not know all the answers to the problems, and should not pretend to do so. But he may be fully assured of the basis of his beliefs.

In general it is to be hoped that where there is a difference of opinion this can be amicable. Unfortunately this is not always the case. It is regrettable that in some situations students are regularly marked down in their essays for accepting a conservative point of view. But it is most important to remember that whatever point of view one accepts, one should know other points of view. If in an essay a student wishes, as a matter of honesty and good conscience, to put a point of view which may not be generally accepted, he should show that he knows the more generally accepted ideas, and also show why he does not accept them. It is hard for any tutor not to give a good mark for such an essay!

Again, it may be a genuine practical problem for the student who accepts the Bible as the Word of God to continue to treat it as such, with all his academic study of it. John Newton gave some advice on this subject 200 years ago, when writing to a student of divinity. Speaking of Scripture and prayer, he said: 'The one is the fountain of living water, the other the bucket with which we are to draw.'[26] The practice of prayer is both the safeguard against spiritual decline and the means of drawing spiritual benefit from what has been studied.

Pannenberg has made some important remarks about theology and doxology, in his *Basic Questions in Theology*: 'Doxology is essentially adoration. In it, as Schlick says, the "I" is sacrificed in the act of praising God Only in this attitude of adoration can God be spoken of in a theological manner.... Only if one keeps in mind that theological statements about God are rooted in adoration can the doctrine of God be protected against false conclusions.'[27]

A FINAL CONSIDERATION

There is a hazard in facing Religious Studies, but it is a hazard which can be accepted. The ultimate question behind all problems faced in Religious Studies is our view of God: we can either think of Him in the biblical way, in theistic terms, as the living God, the supernatural Being, who really is, and who cares, acts and speaks; or we can think of Him in a diminished way, in deistic terms, as One who remotely exists, but does not act directly, only in accordance with and within the laws of nature, and within the limits of natural human ability and comprehension. The God of the Bible is the living God, who confronts us, and makes demands upon us, whom we adore and obey; the other god is made in our image, an object of discussion, who does not disturb us. Here is our basic presupposition in Religious Studies. We can either accept the living God as He is in Scripture, or we can scale Him down to fit in with our own theories. Our decision on this radically affects all our study and all our lives. We need to be warned by Jesus' words to the Sadducees : 'You are mistaken, and surely this is the reason : you do not know either the Scriptures or the power of God.'[28]

The promise of Christ, according to the Fourth Gospel, is : 'If any man is willing to do His will, he shall know. ...'[29] The whole purpose of God's revelation of Himself is, as was pointed out above, for us to obey Him. If we are prepared to obey, then we shall understand. Humble obedience and regular prayer are the Christian's duty, and for these to be effective, a devotional, as well as an academic, reading of Scripture is vital. There need be no conflict in this. Truth discovered in academic study can be used in devotional meditation, prayer and obedience; and investigations into the literary problems of the Gospels, with form criticism and redaction criticism, should lead to a greater understanding, so that the force of the Word of God may be felt as an incentive to Christian living, praying and worshipping.

The student of biochemistry does not cease to eat and enjoy his food because he also studies food; the student of the Scriptures should not cease to feed upon and enjoy them, because he also studies them academically. But this does require a firm resolve. So the Christian can say with the Psalmist, in confidence : 'I have set the Lord always before me; because he is at my right hand, I shall not be moved.'[30] And in all his pursuit of knowledge, his foremost aim will be, with Paul : 'That I may know him'.[31]

Notes

1 Introduction

[1] T. F. Torrance, *God and Rationality* (OUP, 1971), p. 3.
[2] Hywel Jones, *The Doctrine of Scripture Today: Trends in Evangelical Thinking* (Evangelical Press, 1969), pp. 18ff.
[3] Helmut Thielicke, *How Modern Should Theology Be?* (Fontana, 1970), p. 28.
[4] Mark 12:33; Luke 10:27.
[5] 1 Peter 1:13; 3:15.
[6] Harry Blamires, *A Defence of Dogmatism* (SPCK, 1967), p. 3
[7] Heinz Zahrnt, *The Historical Jesus* (Collins, 1963), pp. 132–134.
[8] Harry Blamires, *op. cit*, p. 7.
[9] See Harry Blamires, *The Christian Mind* (SPCK, 1963).
[10] John 16:1, NEB.
[11] Hebrews 1:1f., NEB.
[12] Ephesians 4:14.
[13] Alan Richardson, *Preface to Bible Study* (SCM, 1943), p. 43
[14] E. Stauffer, *New Testament Theology* (SCM, 1955, 1963), p. 175.
[15] Anthony Bloom, *School for Prayer* (Darton, Longman and Todd, 1970), pp. xvf.
[16] Quoted in the preface to Nestle's Greek New Testament (Stuttgart, 1949).
[17] Luke 2:52.

2 Religious Studies

[1] Anselm, *De Divinitatis Essentia*, cap. xiii.
[2] Quoted in Wolfhart Pannenberg, *Basic Questions in Theology* (SCM, 1970), p. 63.
[3] John 14:6.
[4] See J. N. D. Anderson, *Christianity and Comparative Religion* (Tyndale Press, 1970); Lesslie Newbigin, *The Finality of Christ* (SCM, 1969).
[5] Ninian Smart in F. D. Healey (ed.), *Preface to Christian Studies* (Lutterworth, 1971), p. 173.
[6] *Ibid.*, p. 175.
[7] *Ibid.*, p. 176.
[8] *Ibid.*, p. 182.
[9] *Ibid.*, p. 199.
[10] *Ibid.*, p. 204.
[11] *Ibid.*, p. 201.

[12] Alan Richardson, *Preface to Bible Study* (SCM, 1943), p. 34.

3 Modern Approaches

[1] T. F. Torrance, *God and Rationality* (OUP, 1971), p. 6.

[2] *Ibid.*, p. 8.

[3] *Ibid.*, p. 9. See also Michael Polanyi, *Personal Knowledge* (Routledge, 1962), especially chapter 1.

[4] So, *e.g.*, J. A. T. Robinson, *But that I Can't Believe!* (Fontana, 1967).

[5] So, *e.g.*, J. N. D. Anderson, *Christianity: the Witness of History* (Tyndale Press, 1969); C. F. D. Moule, *The Phenomenon of the New Testament* (SCM, 1967); Michael Green, *Man Alive!* (Inter-Varsity Press, 1967).

[6] J. V. Langmead Casserley, *The Retreat from Christianity in the Modern World* (Longmans, 1952), p. 84.

[7] *Ibid.*, p. 81.

[8] *Ibid.*, pp. 81f

[9] Alan Richardson, *The Bible in the Age of Science* (SCM, 1961), p. 98.

[10] *Ibid.*, pp. 105f.; D. Guthrie, *New Testament Introduction* (Tyndale Press, 3rd. ed., 1970), p. 194.

[11] Stephen Neill, *The Interpretation of the New Testament, 1861-1961* (OUP, 1966), pp. 257f.

[12] T. F. Torrance, *op. cit.*, p. 51.

[13] Alistair Kee, *The Way of Transcendence: Christian Faith without Belief in God* (Penguin, 1971), p. 18.

[14] *Ibid.*, p. 21.

[15] In *Theologische Zeitschrift*, vol. 13, pp. 409ff., quoted in in Carl F. H. Henry (ed.), *Jesus of Nazareth: Saviour and Lord* (Tyndale Press, 1966), p. 237.

[16] In *Themelios*, vol. 7, nos. 2/3 (1970), pp. 23–25.

[17] In L. E. Keck and J. L. Martyn (eds.), *Studies in Luke-Acts* (SPCK, 1968), p. 30

[18] C. S. Lewis, *Surprised by Joy* (Fontana, 1959), p. 167.

[19] George A. F. Knight, *A Christian Theology of the Old Testament* (SCM, 1959), p. 20.

[20] Wolfhart Pannenberg, *Basic Questions in Theology* (SCM, 1970), p. 18.

[21] George A. F. Knight, *op. cit.*, p. 116.

[22] *Ibid.*, pp. 230ff.

[23] R. M. Grant, *A Short History of the Interpretation of the Bible* (A. and C. Black, 1965), p. 2.

4 Points of View

[1] Leon Morris, *Studies in the Fourth Gospel* (Paternoster, 1969), p. 9.

[2] *Ibid.*, pp. 10f.

[3] Helmut Thielicke, *How Modern Should Theology Be?* (Fontana, 1970), pp. 82f.

[4] G. W. Anderson, *A Critical Introduction to the Old Testament* (Duckworth, 1959), pp. 7f.

[5] In *Themelios*, vol. 5, no. 2 (1968), p. 5.

[6] Stephen Neill, *The Interpretation of the New Testament, 1861–1961* (OUP, 1966), p. 338.

[7] Helmut Thielicke, *op. cit.*, pp. 89f.

[8] Alan Richardson, *Preface to Bible Study* (SCM, 1943), pp. 22f.

[9] Psalms 114:4; 98:8; Isaiah 55:12.

[10] See R. M. Grant, *A Short History of the Interpretation of the Bible* (A. and C. Black, 1965), p. 64.

5 Miracles

[1] See H. H. Rowley, *The Relevance of the Bible* (James Clarke, 1941), pp. 103ff., and A. M. Hunter, *The Work and Words of Jesus* (SCM, 1950), pp. 54–59.

[2] See Richard Swinburne, *The Concept of Miracle* (Macmillan, 1970) for a discussion of this.

[3] See D. Martyn Lloyd-Jones, *The Supernatural in Medicine* (Christian Medical Fellowship, 1971).

[4] See George A. F. Knight, *A Christian Theology of the Old Testament* (SCM, 1959), p. 222, and Alan Richardson, *Preface to Bible Study* (SCM, 1943) pp. 44ff.

[5] Alan Richardson, *op. cit.*, p. 47.

[6] Wolfhart Pannenberg, *Basic Questions in Theology* (SCM, 1970), p. 75, n. 145.

[7] Rudolf Bultmann, *Jesus Christ and Mythology* (SCM, 1960), pp. 15–17.

[8] Ernst Käsemann, *Essays on New Testament Themes* (SCM, 1964), p. 19.

[9] Reginald H. Fuller, *Interpreting the Miracles* (SCM, 1963,

1966), p. 121.

[10] *Loc. cit.*

[11] Rudolf Bultmann, *op. cit.*, p. 38.

[12] *Ibid.*, pp. 48, 52.

[13] John Macquarrie, *An Existentialist Theology* (SCM, 1953, 1965), pp. 166f.

[14] Bultmann, *op. cit.*, p. 185.

[15] C. F. D. Moule in F. G. Healey (ed.), *Preface to Christian Studies* (Lutterworth, 1971), p. 55.

[16] John Macquarrie, *The Scope of Demythologizing* (SCM, 1960), pp. 12f.

[17] *Ibid.*, pp. 17f.

[18] *Ibid.*, p. 22.

[19] Luke 1:68.

[20] John Macquarrie, *op. cit.*, p. 227.

[21] Alistair Kee, *The Way of Transcendence: Christian Faith without Belief in God* (Penguin, 1971), pp. xi–xix.

[22] C. S. Lewis, *Christian Reflections* (Bles, 1967), pp. 154ff.

[23] Quoted in Carl F. H. Henry (ed.), *Jesus of Nazareth: Saviour and Lord* (Tyndale Press, 1966), p. 65.

[24] Stephen Neill, *The Interpretation of the New Testament, 1861–1961* (OUP, 1966), pp. 9f.

[25] Alan Richardson, *History Sacred and Profane* (SCM, 1964), p. 153.

[26] Alan Richardson, *The Bible in the Age of Science* (SCM, 1961), p. 142.

[27] John Macquarrie, *An Existentialist Theology*, p. 168. See also R. M. Grant, *A Short History of the Interpretation of*

the Bible (A. and C. Black, 1965), p. 164.

[28] John Macquarrie, *The Scope of Demythologizing* p. 239.

[29] 1 Corinthians 9:22.

[30] 1 Corinthians 1:23.

[31] Acts 17.

[32] Herbert Butterfield, *Christianity and History* (1949; Fontana, 1957), pp. 161f.

[33] See above, p. 34.

[34] See above, p. 40.

[35] See T. F. Torrance, *God and Rationality* (OUP, 1971), pp. 11ff.

[36] Alan Richardson, *The Bible in the Age of Science*, p. 106.

[37] M. Polanyi, *Personal Knowledge* (Routledge, 1962), p. 284.

[38] Wolfhart Pannenberg, *Jesus – God and Man* (SCM, 1968), p. 98.

[39] Alan Richardson, *History Sacred and Profane*, p. 186.

[40] Ernst Troeltsch, *The Absoluteness of Christianity* (1901; SCM, 1972), pp. 53, 60.

[41] See Wolfhart Pannenberg, *Basic Questions in Theology* (SCM, 1970), p. 40.

[42] Carl Becker, quoted in Alan Richardson, *History Sacred and Profane*, p. 201.

[43] *Expository Times*, September 1970, p. 381.

6 The Resurrection

[1] 1 Corinthians 15:17.

[2] Stephen Neill, *Interpretation of the New Testament, 1861–1961* (OUP, 1966), p. 288.

[3] Acts 17:32.

[4] 1 Corinthians 15.

[5] On 'The Conception of the Resurrection from the Dead', see Wolfhart Pannenberg, *Jesus – God and Man* (SCM, 1968), pp. 74–88.

[6] John 20:27.

[7] John 20:19.

[8] Clark H. Pinnock in Carl F. H. Henry (ed.), *Jesus of Nazareth: Saviour and Lord* (Tyndale Press, 1966), p. 150.

[9] Ephesians 1: 19, 20.

[10] The English version of Kähler's book is *The So-called Historical Jesus and the Historic, Biblical Christ* (Philadelphia, 1964).

[11] J. A. T. Robinson in a radio broadcast, 20 March 1971.

[12] G. Bornkamm, *Jesus of Nazareth* (Hodder, 1960, 1963), p. 180.

[13] *Ibid.*, pp. 183f.

[14] W. Künneth, *The Theology of the Resurrection* (1933, 1951; SCM, 1965), p. 24.

[15] *Ibid.*, p. 30.

[16] *Ibid.*, p. 33.

[17] Heinz Zahrnt, *The Historical Jesus* (Collins, 1963), pp. 85–87.

[18] *Ibid.*, pp. 88f.

[19] *Ibid.*, p. 133.

[20] *Ibid.*, p. 134.

[21] *Ibid.*, p. 135.

[22] Deuteronomy 8:2.

[23] Exodus 20:2, 3.

[24] See p. 3 above.

[25] See pp. 18f. above.

[26] Paul Tillich, *The Courage to Be* (Fontana, 1962), pp. 171f.

[27] Acts 1:21, 22.

[28] 1 Corinthians 15.

[29] Heinz Zahrnt, *op. cit.*, p. 126.

30 Ibid., p. 126, quoting *The Nature of Faith*, p. 65.

31 H. von Campenhausen, 'The Events of Easter and the Empty Tomb', in *Tradition and Life in the Church* (Collins, 1968), pp. 42–89. See Stephen Neill, *op. cit.*, pp. 286ff., for a discussion of von Campenhausen's work.

32 Wolfhart Pannenberg, *op. cit.*, p. 109.

33 Wolfhart Pannenberg, *Basic Questions in Theology* (SCM, 1970), pp. 37f., 48f., 49, n. 90.

34 Lesslie Newbigin, *Honest Religion for Secular Man* (SCM, 1966), pp. 53–55.

35 Pp. 19f. above.

36 See J. N. D. Anderson, *Christianity: the Witness of History* (Tyndale Press, 1969), chapter 4; C. F. D. Moule, *The Phenomenon of the New Testament* (SCM, 1967).

37 Alan Richardson, *History Sacred and Profane* (SCM, 1964), p. 209. See also John Macquarrie, *An Existentialist Theology* (SCM, 1953, 1965), pp. 186f.

7 Biblical Criticism

1 See chapter 1.

2 Wolfhart Pannenberg, *Basic Questions in Theology* (SCM, 1970), p. 56.

3 Published by the British and Foreign Bible Society, 1958.

4 See G. E. Ladd, *The New Testament and Criticism* (Eerdmans, 1967; Hodder, 1970), p. 93, and chapter 4 on Linguistic Criticism, for examples. See also K. A. Kitchen, *Ancient Orient and Old Testament* (Tyndale Press, 1966), pp. 160ff.

5 See E. J. Carnell, *The Case for Orthodox Theology* (Marshall, Morgan and Scott, 1961), pp. 113f.

6 Vincent Taylor, *The Formation of the Gospel Tradition* (Macmillan, 1935), p. 2.

7 Published in C. S. Lewis, *Christian Reflections* (Bles, 1967), pp. 152ff. See p. 39 above.

8 *Ibid.*, p. 160.

9 See A. S. Peake (ed.), *Commentary on the Bible* (Nelson, 1962), pp. 568f.

10 G. W. Anderson, *A Critical Introduction to the Old Testament* (Duckworth, 1959), p. 7.

11 *Ibid.*, p. 231.

12 *Ibid.*, p. 235.

13 Stephen Neill, *The Interpretation of the New Testament, 1861–1961* (OUP, 1966), p. 346.

14 In L. E. Keck and J. L. Martyn, *Studies in Luke-Acts* (SPCK, 1968), p. 16.

15 K. A. Kitchen, *op. cit.*, p. 101 n. 52.

16 *Loc. cit.*, and p. 128.

17 Genesis 12:10–19 and 20:1–18.

18 Genesis 26:1–14.

19 S. H. Hooke in A. S. Peake (ed.), *Commentary on the Bible*, p. 192, para. 159a.

20 *Loc. cit.*

21 *Ibid.*, p. 290, para. 249j.

22 K. A. Kitchen, *op. cit.*, pp. 116ff.

23 *Ibid.*, p. 121, n. 26.

24 *Ibid.*, pp. 116ff.
25 *Ibid.*, p. 125.
26 M. H. Segal, *The Pentateuch: its composition and its authorship* (Magnes Press, Jerusalem, 1967; distributed by OUP).
27 *Op. cit.*, pp. xi, xii, 2, 4.
28 *Ibid.*, pp. 26f. See also U. Cassuto, *The Documentary Hypothesis* (Magnes Press, Jerusalem, 1961; from OUP).
29 Ivan Engnell, *Critical Essays on the Old Testament* (SPCK, 1970), pp. 3f. See also C. R. North on Pentateuchal Criticism in H. H. Rowley (ed.), *The Old Testament and Modern Study* (OUP, 1951), pp. 48ff.
30 Ivan Engnell, *op. cit.*, p. 4.
31 *Ibid.*, p. 9.
32 *Ibid.*, p. 11.
33 B. Gerhardsson, *Memory and Manuscript* (Uppsala, 1961).
34 Ivan Engnell, *op. cit.*, p. 125.
35 Isaiah 44: 6–8.
36 Norman Porteous, *Daniel: a Commentary* (SCM, 1965).
37 For details, see D. J. Wiseman *et al.*, *Notes on Some Problems in the Book of Daniel* (Tyndale Press, 1965).
38 See Donald Guthrie, *New Testament Introduction* (Tyndale Press, 3rd ed., 1970), p. 208.
39 *Loc. cit.*
40 R. T. Hitt, *Cannibal Valley* (Hodder, 1969), p. 207.
41 Ernst Käsemann, *Essays on New Testament Themes* (SCM, 1964), p. 15.
42 *Ibid.*, pp. 16f.
43 *Ibid.*, p. 62.
44 See J. W. Montgomery in Carl F. H. Henry (ed.), *Jesus of Nazareth: Saviour and Lord* (Tyndale Press, 1966), p. 238.
45 See Donald Guthrie, *op. cit.*, p. 200.
46 Quoted *ibid.*, p. 214, n. 4.
47 See Stephen Neill, *op. cit.*, p. 250.
48 In F. D. Healey (ed.), *Preface to Christian Studies* (Lutterworth, 1971), pp. 49f.
49 Donald Guthrie, *op. cit.*, pp. 189ff.
50 Stephen Neill, *op. cit.*, pp. 247ff.
51 G. E. Ladd, *op. cit.*, p. 163.
52 Vincent Taylor, *op. cit.*, p. 41.
53 Acts 1:21, 22.
54 In F. D. Healey (ed.), *op. cit.*, pp. 49f.
55 See p. 51 above.
56 H. von Campenhausen, *Ecclesiastical Authority and Spiritual Power* (A. and C. Black, 1969), p. 23.
57 *Expository Times*, November 1969, p. 33.
58 G. E. Ladd *op. cit.*, p. 157.
59 *Ibid.*, p. 158.
60 Norman Perrin, *What is Redaction Criticism?* (SPCK, 1970).
61 *Op. cit.*, p. 42.
62 *Op. cit.*, pp. 48ff.
63 *Op. cit.*, p. 53.
64 *Op. cit.*, p. 69.
65 *Op. cit.*, p. 75.
66 *Op. cit.*, p. 73. See also Norman Perrin, *Rediscovering the Teaching of Jesus* (SCM, 1967), pp. 30f.
67 See above, n. 48.
68 B. Gerhardsson, *Memory and Manuscript* (Uppsala, 1961). For Perrin's strictures on this,

see his *Rediscovering the Teaching of Jesus*, pp. 30f.

[69] I. H. Marshall, *Luke: Historian and Theologian* (Paternoster, 1970).

[70] See, *e.g.*, Helmut Thielicke, *How Modern Should Theology Be?* (Fontana, 1970), p. 47.

[71] Norman Perrin, *What is Redaction Criticism?* p. 64.

[72] In F. D. Healey (ed.), *op. cit.*, p. 50.

[73] See pp. 41ff., 48ff. above.

[74] Martin Kähler, *The So-called Historical Jesus and the Historic, Biblical Christ* (1896; Philadelphia, 1964); and see Paul Althaus in Carl F. H. Henry (ed.), *op. cit.*, pp. 201ff.

[75] Reginald H. Fuller, *The New Testament in Current Study* (SCM, 1963), p. 153.

[76] Norman Perrin, *Rediscovering the Teaching of Jesus*, p. 221, and see pp. 50ff. above.

[77] G. Ernest Wright, *God Who Acts* (SCM, 1952), pp. 24, 55.

[78] Stephen Neill, *op. cit.*, p. 285; F. F. Bruce in Carl F. H. Henry (ed.), *op. cit*., p. 89. Leon Morris (concerning the Fourth Gospel, *ibid.* p. 130; W. W. Gasque, in *Themelios* vol. 6, nos. 3/4 (1969).

[79] In Carl F. H. Henry (ed.), *op. cit.*, p. 238.

[80] F. F. Bruce, *ibid.*, p. 89.

[81] A. N. Sherwin-White, *Roman Society and Roman Law in the New Testament* (OUP, 1963), p. 187. See also the discussion of this in E. L. Mascall, *The Secularisation of Christianity* (Darton, Longman and Todd, 1965), pp. 226ff.

[82] Alan Richardson, *History Sacred and Profane* (SCM, 1964).

[83] Wolfhart Pannenberg, *Basic Questions in Theology* (SCM, 1970); see, *e.g.*, pp. 15, 149.

[84] C. F. D. Moule, in F. D. Healey (ed.), *op. cit.*, see, *e.g.*, pp. 52, 55; also his *The Phenomenon of the New Testament* (SCM, 1967).

[85] I. H. Marshall, *op. cit.*

[86] W. O. E. Oesterley and T. H. Robinson, *A History of Israel*, vol. 1 (OUP, 1932) and John Bright, *A History of Israel* (SCM, 1960, 1972).

[87] W. O. E. Oesterley and T. H. Robinson, *op. cit.*, p. 53.

[88] John Bright, *op. cit.*, pp. 63, 68, 69 in the 1960 edition (pp. 70, 75, 76 in the 1972 edition).

[89] G. Ernest Wright, *op. cit.*, pp. 126f.

[90] A. M. Hunter, *The Unity of the New Testament* (SCM, 1943), p. 11.

[91] H. H. Rowley, *The Unity of the Bible* (Lutterworth, 1953, 1967), p. 1.

[92] A. M. Hunter, *op. cit.*, p. 15.

[93] G. W. Anderson, *A Critical Introduction to the Old Testament*, p. 237.

[94] H. H. Rowley, *op. cit.*, p. 7.

[95] George A. F. Knight, *A Christian Theology of the Old Testament* (SCM, 1959), p. 147

[96] G. Ernest Wright, *op. cit.*, p. 35.

[97] H. H. Rowley, *op. cit.*, p. 16.

[98] Alan Richardson, *Preface to Bible Study* (SCM, 1943), p. 43; see also G. A. F. Knight, *op. cit.*, p. 148.

[99] G. W. Anderson, *op. cit.*, p. 7.
[100] In *Themelios*, vol. 5, no. 2 (1968).
[101] H. H. Rowley (ed.), *The Old Testament and Modern Study*, pp. xvii, xviii.
[102] See chapter 4.
[103] Reginald H. Fuller, *op. cit.*, pp. 117, 143.
[104] H. H. Rowley (ed.), *op. cit.*, p. xxx.
[105] In F. D. Healey (ed.), *op. cit.*, p. 56.

8 Disclosure or Discovery

[1] Exodus 3: 11, 12.
[2] See pp. 83f. above.
[3] George A. F. Knight, *A Christian Theology of the Old Testament* (SCM, 1959), p. 148.
[4] English translation published by Harper and Row, New York, 1958.
[5] *Op. cit.*, p. 45.
[6] *Ibid.*, p. 87.
[7] See pp. 80ff. above.
[8] G. Ernest Wright, *God Who Acts* (SCM, 1952).
[9] *Op. cit.*, p. 107.
[10] William Temple, *Nature, Man and God* (Macmillan, 1934).
[11] *Op. cit.*, p. 314.
[12] *Op. cit.*, p. 317.
[13] *Op. cit.*, p. 322.
[14] Wright, *op. cit.* p. 83.
[15] *Ibid.*, p. 84.
[16] John Baillie, *The Idea of Revelation in Recent Thought* (Columbia University Press, New York, 1956).
[17] *Op. cit.*, p. 47.
[18] *Ibid.*, p. 49; see also p. 108.
[19] B. B. Warfield, *The Inspiration and Authority of the Bible* (Marshall, Morgan and Scott, 1951).
[20] John Baillie, *op. cit.*, p. 65.
[21] *Ibid.*, p. 90.
[22] 1 Corinthians 15:3.
[23] John Baillie, *op. cit.*, p. 28.
[24] *Loc. cit.*
[25] James Barr, *The Semantics of Biblical Language* (OUP, 1961), p. 230.
[26] Amos 3:7.
[27] Oscar Cullmann, *Salvation in History* (SCM, 1967), p. 98.
[28] *Ibid.*, p. 89.
[29] George A. F. Knight, *op. cit.*, p. 74.
[30] Wolfhart Pannenberg, *Basic Questions in Theology* (SCM, 1970), p. 25.
[31] Amos 7:14f. and 3:8.
[32] Exodus 4:12.
[33] Numbers 23:5.
[34] See also 2 Samuel 23:2; Jeremiah 1:9; Ezekiel 3:4.
[35] Exodus 24:4.
[36] Joshua 24:26.
[37] Isaiah 30:8.
[38] Nehemiah 8:1.
[39] For a much more detailed examination of the issues involved here, see J. W. Wenham, *Christ and the Bible* (Tyndale Press, 1972).
[40] Matthew 4:4, 7, 10; Deuteronomy 8:3; 6:16; 6:13.
[41] Mark 11: 15–17; Isaiah 56:7; Jeremiah 7:11.
[42] Luke 22: 37; Isaiah 53:12.
[43] Mark 1:15; 'the time is fulfilled'.
[44] Luke 4:21.
[45] John 5:39.
[46] Luke 24:27.
[47] Matthew 19:3–5.

[48] Mark 12:36. On the use of Psalm 110, see R. T. France, *Jesus and the Old Testament* (Tyndale Press, 1971), pp. 163–169.

[49] Mark 12:24–27.

[50] Matthew 5:17, 18.

[51] Matthew 5:21ff.

[52] Luke 16:29–31.

[53] See, *e.g.*, Mark 4:29, from Joel 3:13; Mark 8:18, from Jeremiah 5:21; Mark 9:48, from Isaiah 66:24; and so on.

[54] See, *e.g.*, Mark 1:25–27; 2:1–12; John 7:16; 12:50.

[55] Matthew 1:22; 2:15; 2:17; 2:23; 3:3; 4:14; 8:17; *etc.*

[56] Hebrews 1:1, 2.

[57] Hebrews 3:7, quoting Psalm 95:7; Hebrews 10:15, quoting Jeremiah 31:33.

[58] Romans 9:17.

[59] Galatians 3:8.

[60] For a full discussion of this term, see B. B. Warfield, *op. cit.*, pp. 245–296.

[61] G. W. Anderson, *Critical Introduction to the Old Testament* (Duckworth, 1959), pp. 238f.

[62] John Bright, *The Authority of the Old Testament* (SCM, 1967), p. 77.

[63] John 14:26.

[64] John 16:13, 14.

[65] 1 John 1:1–4.

[66] 1 Thessalonians 2:13; 4:2.

[67] Galatians 1:1, 12.

[68] 1 Corinthians 2:13; 14:37.

[69] See Hebrews 1:1–4; 2:1–4, *etc.*

[70] See p. 89 above.

[71] See pp. 89f. above.

[72] Jude 3.

[73] 2 Thessalonians 2:15.

[74] 1 Timothy 6:20.

[75] 2 Timothy 1:12, 14; 2:2.

[76] 1 Corinthians 2: 9, 10.

[77] A. M. Ramsey, 'The Authority of the Bible' in A. S. Peake (ed.), *Commentary on the Bible* (Nelson, 1962), p. 7.

[78] Quoted in Carl F. H. Henry (ed.), *Jesus of Nazareth; Saviour and Lord* (Tyndale Press, 1966), p. 254.

[79] Quoted in Carl F. H. Henry (ed.) *op. cit.*, p. 256.

[80] Heinz Zahrnt, *The Historical Jesus* (Collins, 1963), p. 30.

[81] *Ibid.*, p. 42.

[82] B. B. Warfield, *op. cit.*, pp. 154–155.

[83] *Loc. cit.*

[84] *Ibid.*, p. 437.

[85] J. I. Packer, *God has Spoken* (Hodder, 1965), p. 15.

[86] Genesis 15:6.

[87] Romans 4:3ff.

[88] Alan Richardson, *Preface to Bible Study* (SCM, 1943), p. 14

[89] *Op. cit.*, pp. 22–23.

[90] See pp. 83ff. and 80 above.

[91] W. H. Venable in *Themelios*, vol. 5, no. 1 (1968), p. 34.

[92] See pp. 55ff. above.

[93] See E. M. B. Green, *The Authority of Scripture* (Falcon, 1963); J. I. Packer, *op. cit.*; G. E. Ladd, *The New Testament and Criticism* (Eerdmans, 1967; Hodder, 1970), especially chapter 1, 'How is the Bible the Word of God?'; R. M. Horn, *The Book that Speaks for Itself* (Inter-Varsity Press, 1969); article 'Inspiration' in *The New Bible Dictionary* (Inter-Varsity Press, 1962); J. W. Wenham, *Christ and the Bible.*

9 O.T. Problems

1 Quoted in R. Davidson, *The Old Testament* (Hodder, 1964), p. 11.
2 John Bowden, *What about the Old Testament?* (SCM, 1969).
3 See, *e.g.*, R. M. Grant, *A Short History of the Interpretation of the Bible* (A. and C. Black, 1965), p. 45; Alan Richardson, *Preface to Bible Study* (SCM, 1943), p. 64; Peter R. Ackroyd, in F. D. Healey (ed.), *Preface to Christian Studies* (Lutterworth, 1971), p. 61; John Bright, *The Authority of the Old Testament* (SCM, 1967), pp. 6ff. (in detail).
4 Peter R. Ackroyd, in F. D. Healey (ed.), *op. cit.*, p. 76.
5 See, *e.g.*, Wolfhart Pannenberg, *Basic Questions in Theology* (SCM, 1970), *passim*.
6 See chapter 7, n. 91.
7 G. Ernest Wright, *God who Acts* (SCM, 1952), p. 19.
8 See John Bright, *op. cit.*, chapter 4.
9 G. Ernest Wright, *op. cit.*, p. 21.
10 R. M. Grant, *op. cit.*, p. 59.
11 George A. F. Knight, *A Christian Theology of the Old Testament* (SCM, 1959), p. 21.
12 *Ibid.*, p. 74.
13 G. Ernest Wright, *op. cit.*, pp. 49f.
14 Immanuel Kant, *Prolegomena to any Future Metaphysic* (1783; Liberal Arts Press edition, USA, 1950), p. 105.
15 John Bright, *op. cit.*, pp. 77f.
16 Derek Kidner, *Hard Sayings; The challenge of Old Testament morals* (Inter-Varsity Press, 1972).
17 *Op. cit.*, p. 7.
18 *Op. cit.*, pp. 22–25.
19 George A. F. Knight, *op. cit.*, p. 86.
20 *Ibid.*, p. 122.
21 Alan Richardson, *op. cit.*, p. 72.
22 Exodus 21:23f.
23 Matthew 5:38ff.
24 Hebrews 11:32.
25 See pp. 108f. above.
26 H. H. Rowley, *The Unity of the Bible* (Lutterworth, 1953, 1967), p. 15.
27 See pp. 35ff. above.
28 E. L. Mascall, *Christian Theology and Natural Science* (Longmans, 1956, 1957), pp. 155ff.
29 See D. C. Spanner, *Creation and Evolution* (Falcon, 1965).
30 See chapters 5 and 6.
31 See chapter 8.
32 Genesis 1:26.
33 Genesis 1:31.
34 2 Corinthians 4:4.

10 Christ and Criticism

1 Heinz Zahrnt, *The Historical Jesus* (Collins, 1963), p. 142.
2 P. N. Hamilton, 'Some Proposals for a Modern Christology' in *Christ for us Today, Papers from the Fiftieth Annual Conference of Modern Churchmen, 1967* (SCM, 1968).
3 *Op. cit.*, p. 155.
4 *Ibid.*, p. 161.
5 *Ibid.*, p. 165.
6 *Ibid.*, p. 175.
7 Isaiah 55:8f.
8 C. S. Lewis, *Christian Reflections* (Bles, 1967), p. 165.
9 Reginald H. Fuller, *The*

Foundations of New Testament Christology (Lutterworth, 1965; Fontana, 1969).

[10] Oscar Cullmann, *The Christology of the New Testament* (SCM, 1959).

[11] Carl F. H. Henry (ed.), *Jesus of Nazareth: Saviour and Lord* (Tyndale Press, 1966).

[12] C. F. D. Moule, *The Phenomenon of the New Testament* (SCM, 1967).

[13] I. H. Marshall, 'The Development of Christology in the Early Church', *Tyndale Bulletin* 18 (1967), and *Luke, Historian and Theologian* (Paternoster, 1970).

[14] Hans Conzelmann, *An Outline of the Theology of the New Testament* (SCM, 1969).

[15] Joachim Jeremias, *New Testament Theology* (SCM, 1971).

[16] Reginald H. Fuller, *op. cit.*, p. 15

[17] J. V. Langmead Casserley, *The Retreat from Christianity in the Modern World* (Longmans, 1952), chapter 4.

[18] Reginald H. Fuller, *op. cit.*, p. 17.

[19] I. H. Marshall, 'The Development of Christology in the Early Church', p. 5.

[20] *Op. cit.*, p. 205.

[21] *Ibid.*, pp. 247f.

[22] Stephen Neill, *The Interpretation of the New Testament, 1861–1961* (OUP, 1966), p. 182.

[23] *Ibid.*, pp. 185f.

[24] In F. D. Healey (ed.), *op. cit.*, pp. 36f.

[25] A. M. Hunter, *The Unity of the New Testament* (SCM, 1943), p. 34.

[26] *Ibid.*, p. 37

[27] See E. L. Mascall, *The Secularisation of Christianity* (Darton, Longman and Todd, 1965), pp. 228f.; and I. H. Marshall, *op. cit.*, pp. 9f.

[28] Reginald H. Fuller, *op. cit.*, p. 18.

[29] See Joachim Jeremias, *op. cit.*, pp. 1–2; G. E. Ladd, *The New Testament and Criticism* (Eerdmans, 1967; Hodder, 1970), p. 164.

[30] Reginald H. Fuller, *op. cit.*, p. 116.

[31] *Ibid.*, p. 123.

[32] *Ibid.*, p. 130.

[33] In *Themelios*, vol. 3, no. 2 (1966), p. 30.

[34] Reginald H. Fuller, *op. cit.*, p. 121.

[35] Morna D. Hooker, *The Son of Man in Mark* (SPCK, 1967).

[36] C. Colpe, in G. Kittel, *Theological Dictionary of the New Testament* (trans. G. Bromiley, Eerdmans, 1964–).

[37] Norman Perrin, *Rediscovering the Teaching of Jesus* (SCM, 1967).

[38] Hans Conzelmann, *op. cit.*, pp. 131–137.

[39] Norman Perrin, *What is Redaction Criticism?* (SPCK, 1970), p. 70.

[40] Joachim Jeremias, *op. cit.*, p. 37.

[41] Reginald H. Fuller, *op. cit.*, pp. 114f.

[42] Acts 7:56.

[43] See Morna D. Hooker, *op. cit.*, pp. 182ff.

[44] See C. F. D. Moule's 'Christology of Acts', in

L. E. Keck and J. L. Martyn (eds.), *Studies in Luke-Acts* (SPCK, 1968), pp. 159ff.

45 I. H. Marshall, *Luke, Historian and Theologian*, pp. 166f.

46 Luke 24: 34.

47 Eduard Schweizer, *Jesus* (SCM, 1971), chapter 2.

48 C. F. D. Moule, *The Phenomenon of the New Testament*, p. 53.

49 See Joachim Jeremias, *New Testament Theology*, vol. 1, pp. 61–68 (a summary); *The Central Message of the New Testament* (SCM, 1965); and, for full details, *The Prayers of Jesus* (SCM, 1967).

50 Galatians 4:6; Romans 8:15.

51 C. F. D. Moule, *op. cit.*, p. 68.

52 H. Schlier, in G. Kittel, *Theological Dictionary of the New Testament*.

53 Matthew 11: 28.

54 Reginald H. Fuller, *Interpreting the Miracles* (SCM, 1963).

55 Reginald H. Fuller, *The Foundations of New Testament Christology*, p. 257.

56 C. F. D. Moule, *op. cit.*, p. 47.

11 Practical Issues

1 John Bowden, *What about the Old Testament?* (SCM, 1969), p. 113.

2 *Ibid.*, pp. 114, 117.

3 A. M. Ramsey, 'The Authority of the Bible', in A. S. Peake (ed.), *Commentary on the Bible* (Nelson, 1962), p. 5.

4 John Bright, *The Authority of the Old Testament* (SCM, 1967), p. 156.

5 *Ibid.*, p. 38.

6 C. F. D. Moule, *The Birth of the New Testament* (A. and C. Black, 1962, 1966), p. 188.

7 See chapter 8.

8 2 Timothy 3:16.

9 M. R. James, *The Apocryphal New Testament* (OUP, 1924).

10 C. F. D. Moule, *op. cit.*, p. 192.

11 John Bright, *op. cit.*, p. 159.

12 Hebrews 1:1f.

13 G. E. Ladd, *The New Testament and Criticism* (Eerdmans, 1967; Hodder, 1970), p. 21.

14 Deuteronomy 29:29.

15 2 Timothy 3:16f.

16 George A. F. Knight, *A Christian Theology of the Old Testament* (SCM, 1959), p. 17.

17 See chapter 10.

18 1 Corinthians 11:6.

19 2 Corinthians 4:6.

20 John 16:12–14.

21 Oscar Cullmann, *The Earliest Christian Confession* (Lutterworth, 1949), pp. 27, 58.

22 J. B. Phillips, *The Ring of Truth* (Hodder, 1967), p. 12.

23 Isaiah 6.

24 John 17:3.

25 See E. L. Mascall, *Christian Theology and Natural Science* (Longmans, 1956, 1957), p. 96.

26 Quoted in *Themelios*, vol. 2, no. 2 (1964).

27 Wolfhart Pannenberg, *Basic Questions in Theology* (SCM, 1970), pp. 203, 216.

28 Mark 12: 24, NEB.

29 John 7: 17.

30 Psalm 16:8.

31 Philippians 3:10.